Changing Perspectives on Benefit Take-up

S P R U

SOCIAL POLICY RESEARCH UNIT

First published 1995

ISBN 0 11 701875 9

This paper is based on work funded by the Department of Social Security but the opinions expressed are those of the researcher alone.

Editor for this paper: Peter Whiteford

British Library Cataloguing in Publication Data

A CIP catalogue entry for this book is available from the British Library.

Acknowledgements

This paper is based on work commissioned by the Benefits Agency from the Social Policy Research Unit.

In developing her ideas the author has benefited from discussions over the years with Robert Walker. Recent opportunities to share views with Wim van Oorschot have been especially valuable.

John Ditch and Peter Whiteford kindly commented on draft versions of the manuscript, and Lorna Foster and Sally Pulleyn provided essential technical support.

Contents

Why another review?

The importance of take-up

Issues concerning take-up have remained high on the social security research agenda for nearly four decades. The term describes the process of claiming entitlements to benefits and allowances. In addition, when used as a quantified outcome measure, a take-up estimate represents that proportion of overall entitlement actually received, or the percentage of people entitled who receive benefit.

Interest in take-up (more specifically, interest in *non*-take-up) arose as a consequence of research on poverty during the 1950s and early 1960s (Corden, 1983; Craig, 1991). Put simply, it became clear that many poor people were not receiving benefits and services available to them. Had they claimed their entitlements, some people, in particular elderly people and families with children, might have raised their income level and enjoyed higher standards of living.

This association with impoverishment has continued to focus attention on take-up from policy makers and social policy analysts. The introduction of new income-related benefits in the 1970s, and new benefits to help meet the extra costs of disability and caring, brought new groups of people and sets of circumstances under the spotlight. At a local level interest was translated into action, and welfare rights activity, combining advice, advocacy and campaigning roles, emerged as a new sector of welfare provision, to promote take-up both of centrally provided social security, and locally administered services and subsidies.

Alongside interest in the scale of non-take-up came the need to develop techniques of measurement and quantification. Recent concern about the growth in social security expenditure (DSS, 1993a) has increased the urgency of the Government's need for reliable estimates of take-up. The Treasury requires accurate forecasts of potential eligibility and receipt, both under current arrangements and when planning changes in the rules governing eligibility or the introduction of new schemes.

More fundamentally, measures of take-up provide indicators of effectiveness in implementing social security policy. As the Government's aim in the overall social security programme is increasingly expressed in terms of targeting resources effectively on the most needy in society (DHSS, 1985) so there is increased interest in measures which demonstrate relative success in hitting the targets. Thus the take-up measure of a benefit such as family credit is available for critical assessment of the success of policy designed to target resources at families with children. In so far as an additional policy aim of that benefit is to maintain incentives to work, the take-up measure provides an indication of the extent to which low-income families understand and respond to the apparent incentive.

Along with its function as an indicator of effectiveness in social security policy, van Oorschot (1991) sees the take-up measure as an indicator of social justice. If non-take-up means that people are deprived of their rights and entitlements, he argues, then the resulting injustice is a cause for concern. He sees the social security system as a key institution for the promotion of a just distribution of resources to people whose eligibility defines their insufficient share. There are, of course, inherent ideological contradictions here between this kind of argument and recent policy development emphasising individual responsibility, consumerism and choice (Taylor-Gooby, 1994). The language of the 1985 reform of the British social security system was not primarily one of social justice. However, whether or not we choose to associate take-up with social justice, there is no doubt about the importance attached to it.

As we would expect, there is a wide and interesting body of literature and research addressing the measurement of take-up, the determinants of claiming behaviour and the reduction of non-take-up.

Reviewing research on take-up

A major review of research on take-up of income-related benefits was conducted by Craig in 1991 with a view to identifying the most promising lines of future enquiry. Craig discusses aspects of the measurement of take-up, and goes on to discuss the factors affecting take-up. He discusses the development of models of the claiming process, and describes alternative econometric approaches which use continuous survey data. He focuses on some of the problems facing take-up research, especially that of sampling eligible non-recipients, and concludes by examining various options for identifying such groups. In the light of this recent important review article, readers may wonder why there is scope for another review.

Craig chose to restrict the scope of his review – first, by looking at take-up from the research perspective rather than that of policy, and secondly, by concentrating on claiming decisions rather than benefit delivery. The latter distinction is artificial, however, as Craig acknowledged. Attitudes and feelings that affect claiming decisions are influenced by aspects of organisational structure and administration at various levels. If 'demand' for benefits is constrained by 'supply' (Craig, 1991, p. 538) then we may expect this to affect take-up.

The aim of this paper is to revisit the take-up literature from the perspective of 'supply', in order to fill some of the gaps left by Craig, as well as including material published more recently. Taking a broader perspective helps to widen the debate on the concept of take-up and raises interesting issues about the validity of its traditional status in the evaluation of social security policy.

The following section argues that, although models of the claiming process have proved useful, the impact made by those grounded in individual claimant decision making (on which Craig focuses) has perhaps diverted attention from other models that emphasise the organisational structure within which claiming decisions are made. Three such 'alternative' schemes are presented and from these, the one derived from comparative European study provides a framework for subsequent discussion. The following chapters then address take-up within the context of, first, structural aspects of benefit design, and secondly, practical aspects of benefit administration. Essential aspects of process that are increasingly recognised as important emerge from the discussion, such as time parameters and errors in adjudication. The final chapter suggests that despite the status of take-up as an evaluative indicator, and the research attention it has attracted, the concept has been narrowly based. The need now may be to move towards a broader approach.

The literature reviewed has all been published (unless otherwise indicated, in a small number of cases). Other relevant literature is produced during the Department of Social Security's internal monitoring and evaluation of benefits, such as form design developmental work. This work is not widely disseminated, although sometimes made available on request. For practical reasons, the review has not attempted to include this type of literature. Nor has there been any attempt to evaluate the methodology of the research reported. It has been assumed that findings discussed here are based on work that has been appropriately designed and conducted.

Individualistic models of the claiming process

Craig described and compared the two most influential models of the claiming process, both developed in the early 1980s (Craig, 1991). These were Kerr's 'threshold model' (Kerr, 1982, 1983) developed to investigate the differential take-up of supplementary pension, and a 'trade-off model' (Ritchie and Matthews, 1982) originally used in a study of rent allowances. Kerr was primarily interested in why some pensioners failed to claim the means-tested pension to which they were entitled. His approach was to look for psychological determinants of claiming behaviour – the beliefs, attitudes and feelings of the individual elderly person. His systematic organisation of six constructs of claiming behaviour into a model that could be tested and used both interpretatively and predictively was an exciting development. A number of other studies on means-tested benefits incorporated elements of Kerr's model into design and analytic stages, as described by Craig (for example Corden, 1983, 1987a; Graham, 1984; Davies and Ritchie, 1988). Millar and Cooke (1984) used the model in research on a non-means-tested benefit, one-parent benefit, and Corden (1987b) suggested that Kerr's model might be useful in understanding the non-take-up of disability benefits.

The immediate impact of Kerr's model reflects to some extent the stagnation that the take-up debate had reached. Craig explains why the model broke new ground and stimulated fresh thinking, being 'an ingenious attempt to cut through the conceptual clutter which affected take-up research by the late 1970s' (Craig, 1991, p. 544). From this distance the limitations of the model are not difficult to spot. For example, it does not accommodate easily effects on claiming of interactions between household members, or the sequential aspects of pursuing an application. Ritchie and Matthews were aware that both these latter aspects could be important and pursued them in their research interviews (Ritchie and Matthews, 1982, p. 12). They were developing their own model of stages in the decision making process at the same time as Kerr was working on his, and had discussed the trade-off process with him. In the same way as Kerr's, their eventual model was also grounded mainly in the beliefs, expectations and attitudes of the individual claimant, and choices made between alternative strategies.

It is useful to look for reasons for the subsequent dominance of these models of individual choice and decision making. They have been used extensively to explain the process of claiming and have had a powerful influence on the concept of take-up itself. There were, as described in the following section, alternative models being developed in the 1980s – models which incorporated and gave importance to structural and administrative features as well as individual decision making. In addition, as discussed later, there was evidence from welfare rights activity throughout the 1980s demonstrating clearly how take-up could be influenced dramatically by 'supply side' initiatives that required minimal individual decision making by claimants. Yet it is the two individualistic models of claiming behaviour that are most widely known, and their influence persists (see, for example, Huby and Dix, 1992). Craig is right to emphasise the kick-start that these models gave to the development of research on take-up, but there are likely to be other factors which help explain why it went so far in the same direction.

First, the models are firmly based within the ideology of individualism – an approach to explaining and interpreting events and circumstances mainly in terms of attitudes, decision making and behaviour of the individuals involved. The dominance of individualism within western capitalist culture is discussed by Howe (1990) in the context of his study of the claiming behaviour of unemployed men, and further perspectives are offered by Jordan *et al.* (1992) in the context of relationships in households with unemployed heads. It is a pervasive theme in every facet of life, and is routinely used to explain how society works (Hutson and Jenkins, 1989). It is an ideology firmly espoused and supported by recent Conservative Governments. The Government was a major commissioner of research on take-up during the 1980s, and would tend naturally to be interested in models of the claiming process that did not challenge predominant ideology.

A second possible reason to explain the influence of the Kerr-type models is that research on take-up has been dominated by studies of non-take-up by eligible people. Kerr's model was specifically designed to investigate this aspect of claiming behaviour and, indeed, is less successful at picking claimants than non-claimants when used predictively (Davies and Ritchie, 1988). It is non-take-up by eligible people that has been the main focus of policy interest until recently, both as a result of the association of non-take-up with poverty and low standards of living, and because of the increasing importance of encouraging take-up of in-work means-tested benefits throughout the 1970s and 1980s. McLaughlin *et al.* (1990) argue that 'an essentially pragmatic approach towards take-up (what can be done to ameliorate low take-up)' has developed (p. 1). They point out that unsuccessful claiming by ineligible people has been almost entirely ignored until recently, although this is as common, if not more so, as delayed take-up or non-claiming by eligible people across a number of means-tested and non-means-tested benefits. The policy implications of 'take-up' by ineligible people are important. Applications from ineligible people compete with those from people with entitlements in terms of attention from the administrators – they fill the telephone switchboards and lengthen the processing time. Delays experienced or anticipated by eligible applicants depress take-up and administrative costs are inflated. Moreover, people's circumstances change – ineligible people turn into people with entitlements, but experiences of previous rejections may deter new applications. So it is important to look across the whole spectrum of claiming behaviour and eligibility status. Indeed, McLaughlin et al. make the interesting suggestion that by ignoring the extent and significance of applications from ineligible people, we tend to overstate the resistance to state provision of welfare. This may in turn help to legitimate a view that state welfare is moral anathema to large numbers of people, increasing the association with stigma (McLaughlin *et al.*, 1990).

Corden's study of failed applications for family income supplement (Corden, 1987a) was one of the first academic studies to focus on take-up in a broader sense. Results demonstrated the influence of administrative procedure. More recently, McLaughlin (1991) studied unsuccessful claims for invalid care allowance alongside successful claims from eligible people. She found a poor fit with the Kerr-type claiming model and called for a broader conceptualisation of 'claiming' (McLaughlin *et al.*, 1990).

Turning to the literature on economic approaches to studying take-up, reviewed by Craig, we find little emerging from the early work that questioned the influence of the Kerr-type model. While this may be partly due to reluctance of social researchers and economists to stray across academic boundaries (Craig, 1991), it seems likely that there are other factors as well. Much of the economic work is also underpinned by theory that lies within the ideology of individualism, emphasising choice and behaviour based on conventional notions of utility maximisation. For example, much of the early work was concerned with modelling stigma as a psychological cost in the demand for benefits (Weisbrod, 1970; Moffitt, 1983; Cowell, 1986). 'Supply side' variables proved hard to quantify, and claiming behaviour of ineligible people received almost no attention from the economists. In the more recent economic work on take-up, however, attention has started to move towards the significance of administrative factors (Blundell *et al.*, 1988; Dorsett and Heady, 1991; Duclos, 1992; Noble *et al.*, 1992; Fry and Stark, 1993) and we return to such work later in the paper.

A final suggestion, in the search for reasons for the influence of the Kerr-type model, is that much research and policy analysis during the 1980s set take-up closely alongside issues to do with incentives to work. The in-work benefits, family credit (and its predecessor family income supplement), housing benefit, and more recently disability working allowance are designed against a background of labour supply theory. Craig suggested that there might be considerable advantages in placing take-up research within wider frameworks of household economic choices (Craig, 1991). One disadvantage, however, may be to reinforce an emphasis on understanding, identification and decision making at the level of the individual, and to obscure a need for a broader conceptualisation of take-up. Constructs in Kerr's model such as perception of eligibility or perceived stability of circumstances fit fairly comfortably alongside constructs such as 'income risk'. 'Trade-offs' and 'better-off situations' are common to both Kerr-type models and explanations of labour supply. A process of reinforcement by shared terminology may have helped to maintain the profile of the individualistic claiming models, and diverted attention from alternatives that might have widened the concept of take-up. The following sections look at three alternative models, which take greater account of structural organisation and administrative process.

Alternative models incorporating structure and administration

There have been three main attempts to move away from concentrating on the psychological determinants of individual claiming behaviour towards models that recognise 'supply side' factors.

An early attempt by Walker (1980) has recently been revised and developed to attempt to capture more accurately the dynamics of information flow and temporal aspects of the claiming process (Vincent *et al.*, 1991). Walker's original model drew on contemporary literature on information-seeking and use (Rogers with Shoemaker, 1971; Donohew *et al.*, 1978). Within an information environment which is constantly changing and likely to include disinformation, individuals' information needs also change according to context and circumstance.

The updated version models the search for information. A series of recursive stages is proposed, during which the information environment may be sampled in different ways: pre-awareness, awareness, search, consultation, decision, application and outcome. The outcome of the application is unlikely to be an end state, but successful and unsuccessful applicants monitor the new situation and may return to earlier stages. Changes in individual circumstances and in the benefit system will act to make the situation unstable.

An advantage of this approach is that attention is focused on the information environment, its structure, and the content and availability of information 'rather than placing the burden of responsibility overwhelmingly on the potential applicant' (Vincent *et al.*, 1991, p. 16). By focusing on the dynamics of information needs, some insight can be gained into unsuccessful claiming – the utility of information changes as decisions are taken and situations alter. The model is not yet tested, but the authors suggest that this type of process model has more general application across a range of benefits and clients than the Kerr-type model, which has been found to work better for some benefits than others, and may describe the experiences of pensioners more accurately than those of other groups. A further advantage claimed for this approach is that it offers more opportunities for understanding possible intervention strategies to make the application process easier.

A second reappraisal of the Kerr-type model of the claiming process comes from Buckland and Dawson (1989). They argue that individual claims should be examined within the context of household decision making. Such decisions are influenced by complex factors within and outside the households at each event in the life history of a claim. This complex process is not captured within the individualistic model of claiming, and a broader model provides a more useful framework.

Buckland and Dawson suggest a scheme incorporating a number of distinct changes associated with the lifecycle of specific claims: conception, preparation, assessment, consideration of outcome and routine claiming. The model accounts for the sequential nature of claiming, and accommodates effects of intra-household decision making, response and initiatives of the Department of Social Security (DSS), and the possibility of a single household being at different stages in the lifecycle of separate applications at any one time. Buckland and Dawson applied the model in a study of 50 low-income households in the context of claiming supplementary benefit.

Buckland and Dawson claim, as did Walker, that this broader non-individualistic approach can suggest strategies for intervention that might improve take-up. They argue that little attention has been paid so far to combatting obstacles to claiming associated with the later stages in the claiming process. Many strategies for improving take-up still centre on the dissemination of information to potential claimants about their eligibility – the 'conception state' in their model. The possibilities of intervention at later stages are developed further when Dawson, Buckland and Gilbert go on to discuss how new computer technology could provide opportunities for developing welfare advice systems (Dawson *et al.*, 1990). Later chapters discuss various aspects of opportunities provided by new technology.

The final model described here emerged from an international review of European data and research on take-up (van Oorschot and Kolkhuis Tancke, 1989). Van Oorschot's critique of the Kerr model (van Oorschot, 1991; van Oorschot and Schell, 1991) is directed at two main weaknesses. First, the analysis is confined to the client level, and second, within this level it is limited to only one aspect of claiming behaviour – not putting in a claim at all.

Van Oorschot suggests major adjustments to the Kerr-type model in order to represent the process of decision making about claiming. He retains elements of both the 'threshold' and 'trade-off' ideas from previous individualistic models. Two constructs with a threshold character are basic knowledge and perceived eligibility. These are combined with a trade-off between promoting and deterring factors, which include perceptions of need, utility and the stability of the situation, as well as attitudes to dependency on welfare, the benefit in question and the perceived nature and consequences of the administrative process. However, 'trigger events' can be additional factors in this model. These can act directly on decisions to claim, as might happen when somebody was told to claim, in effect, short-circuiting the decision making process. Trigger events might also act indirectly, however, by altering the relative weights of promoting or deterring factors. For example, arrival of an unexpectedly large bill might alter the relative importance of factors subjected to a trade-off, say need and negative feelings about financial assistance. This might then lead to information-seeking and sufficient confidence in eligibility to make a claim.

Van Oorschot prefers to see this scheme as an heuristic tool for future research, rather than a total causal model. The scheme suggests that there are a number of different paths to the decision to claim, with or without trigger events. It is useful for representing what may happen in delayed claims, or when negative attitudes inhibit reception of relevant information. One way of testing van Oorschot's three-t-model (threshold – trade-off – trigger) would be to follow claimants over a period of time.

While this model may be useful as an heuristic tool for further research, of greater significance for this paper is van Oorschot's emphasis on the different levels at which factors affecting take-up can be distinguished analytically. Factors at the client level are of critical importance, of course, and he urges further testing and refinement of models of decision making, such as his proposed three-t-model. However, it is not enough, he argues, to look solely at the motives, intentions and decisions of applicants themselves.

Policy makers and administrators have equally significant roles at different levels of influence. The design of the benefit is the province of the policy makers. Elements of design, including the eligibility criteria and requirements for demonstrating entitlement, the name of the benefit, the amount of money available and length of award, and the position of the benefit within the overall social security system, are all likely to have some effect on take-up.

In between the policy maker and the claimant is the administration, and at this level the way in which benefits are delivered is also likely to have some influence. As a result of an international review of take-up research, van Oorschot and Kolkhuis Tancke (1989) constructed an inventory organising the factors affecting take-up at three levels of classification:

- the benefit scheme
- the administration, and
- the client.

At the time of writing, this attempt at a systematic classification of influences on take-up, giving structural and administrative factors equal status with the claimant experience, was currently a theoretical development. (Van Oorschot was testing parts of both the three-t-model and the three level schema, and a forthcoming publication will describe his results (van Oorschot, 1995).) Although at a theoretical stage, the schema was useful in establishing a framework for presentations of 'supply-side' effects on take-up in this review. Supply side factors are essentially those to do with benefit design and administration.

The following chapters are thus organised to look at research and literature, first, about the effects of benefit structure, and then about the effects of procedure and administration in delivering benefits. Adopting parts of van Oorschot's schema for a presentational framework also provides opportunities to explore how appropriate this approach may be for the British social security system.

Structure of the review

One of the aims of the first chapter was to remind readers why take-up remains high on the list of priorities for research and discussion. This review takes a different perspective from that adopted by Craig in an earlier article, and by revisiting the literature from the 'supply side', fills some of the gaps which Craig chose to leave. Three 'models' or schemas offer alternatives to previous individualistic models of the decision making process. The parameters of these models are different. Vincent *et al.* model the search for benefit information; Buckland and Dawson model the claiming process; van Oorschot presents a classification of factors affecting take-up, in which he locates a model of decision making at the client level. The models are all useful in different ways, and have all influenced the framework for the following discussion. Van Oorschot's classification, setting structural and administrative influences alongside the claimant experience, seems particularly useful for our purpose here.

The review looks first, in Chapter Two, at what is known about the effects on take-up of benefit structure. The following chapters are concerned with administrative effects on take-up. Chapter Three looks at information supply, and Chapter Four examines practical aspects of service provision, including location and staffing of points of access for claimants and means of communication with administrative staff. Chapter Five is concerned with procedural aspects of making an application for benefit, accuracy of decision making and aspects of policing the system. Chapter Six concludes by suggesting that the perspective gained by focusing on supply side factors demonstrates a need to widen the concept of take-up itself.

Effects on take-up of benefit structure

In terms of efficiency, effectiveness and social justice, the aim is for benefits to reach all those with entitlement, with minimum levels of applications from and awards to ineligible people. (There can be interesting 'perverse incentives' here, however, for example where administrative performance indicators include a target for refusals, as has been the case for unemployment benefit (Harper, 1993).) Whether such a goal can be achieved seems likely to depend partly on the design and characteristics of the benefit concerned. One of the main themes of a national conference convened to consider the welfare rights campaigns of the early 1980s was that low take-up rates have much to do with the structural organisation of the benefit system itself (Hill and Maunders, 1983).

From their international review of take-up research van Oorschot and Kolkhuis Tancke (1989) found a greater probability of non-take-up in schemes that:

- have a high density of rules and guidelines
- contain complex rules
- contain vague criteria of entitlement
- contain a means test
- are aimed at groups in society which are the subject of negative valuation (associated with negative prejudices)
- supplement other sources of income
- leave the initiative to start the claiming process fully to the applicant.

As this initial attempt to systematise structural effects leading to low take-up was derived from an international review, there is unlikely to be a complete fit with the British experience. It is possible, however, to look for supporting evidence from the British social security system. The rest of this section reviews research findings that are relevant to each of the characteristics of benefits identified by van Oorschot and Kolkhuis Tancke (summarised in English by van Oorschot, 1991) and suggests other features that might be added to their list.

Density of rules and guidelines, and complexity of rules

Van Oorschot does not define either 'density' or 'complexity' in the first two criteria mentioned. Clearly, there is likely to be some overlap – benefits that have lots of rules may seem complicated because of this, even if each separate rule is fairly simple.

The number and complexity of rules and guidelines for disability benefits have long been identified from results of local surveys and welfare initiatives as a major barrier to take-up (for example, Casserley and Clark, 1977; Cohen, 1983; DHSS, 1984; Day, 1985; Hardie and Miller, 1985). Recent qualitative research with disabled people (Hedges and Thomas, 1994) has led to a conclusion that the structure of the overall disability benefits system inhibits take-up. This conclusion is supported by interviews conducted by Costigan, Ritchie and White (1992). In a system where eligibility for different benefits depends on the type and severity of disablement and/or the extent and type of care needed, Costigan *et al.* conclude that it is unlikely that people will be able properly to recognise their eligibility without a great deal of help and advice.

The more precisely targeted a means-tested benefit, the greater the complexity of rules is likely to be, to make sure it reaches the target population. This was adopted at an early stage as part of the general case against selective benefits (Hill, 1976). As an example of a precisely targeted means-tested benefit, family credit is designed to boost low earnings of working parents. Entitlement depends on a complex permutation of number of children, ages of children, hours of work, savings and net income. Each of the latter three components has its own schedule of rules for definition and determination. Research on family credit and its predecessor family income supplement has repeatedly shown that this level of complexity is too great to be assimilated by many people in the potential population. The effect, in delaying and preventing applications, inhibiting appeals and contributing to the dissemination of misinformation can be to depress take-up (Corden, 1983, 1987a; Corden and Craig, 1991; Boden and Corden, 1994).

Vague criteria of entitlement

It is a paradox that precise and complex rules of entitlement have to be summarised or reformulated in general terms for promotional purposes, creating, in turn, an apparent imprecision or, in the terminology used by van Oorschot, 'vagueness'. As an example, family credit is promoted as available to 'families on low earnings' in an effort to encapsulate some of the complexity of the income requirement. Such an imprecise concept prevents people identifying themselves as included and the effect on depressing take-up is described in research by Corden *et al.* previously cited. A further effect of imprecision in eligibility criteria is that ineligible people are encouraged to apply. While these effects have traditionally been interpreted at the client level in terms of misunderstanding, or inability to make the necessary intellectual links, they may be equally well interpreted in terms of the characteristics of the benefit itself.

The eligibility criteria for family credit are not really 'vague'. It is the need to promote a benefit of extreme precision in popular terms that produces the 'vagueness'. A different kind of 'imprecision' is attached to benefits that incorporate considerable discretion in entitlement criteria.

The concept of take-up is hard to address in discretionary schemes (Whyley and Huby, 1993). How is the potential population or the 'accuracy' of decision making to be determined (Walker, Dix and Huby, 1992)? There can be measurement of eligibility to apply, but not of entitlement. Research on the social fund shows that the lack of apparent consistency in patterns of adjudication makes it difficult for potential applicants to evaluate their chances of success. More than half the group of eligible non-applicants identified in an evaluation of the social fund said they would not expect to get help from that source (Huby and Dix, 1992, Table 11.18). The overall finding of that evaluation was that there was no evidence from the data to suggest that needs and circumstances of those who received awards were different from those refused. Such a finding is important in a broad conceptualisation of take-up. The design of the social fund, mixing discretionary decisions about entitlement with a cash-limited budget, is unique in British social policy and has attracted controversy and criticism. Several research reports have linked inequities in access and distribution with the unusual structural features (for example, Barnardos, 1990; Smith, 1990; NACAB, 1991; NAO, 1991a; Cohen *et al.*, 1992; Craig, 1992).

A means-test

Interest in non-take-up arose primarily from studies of people in populations entitled to means-tested benefits, and has been fuelled by the general policy direction towards selectivity. The deterrent effect of the means-test has received much attention. There has long been broad agreement that means-testing is linked with the problem of stigmatisation (Titmuss, 1968; Pinker, 1971; Davies and Reddin, 1978).

Stigmatisation is a complex topic engaging sociologists, psychologists and political scientists, as well as those in the social policy arena. An overview of relevant theoretical perspectives on stigmatisation and means-testing is presented by van Oorschot and Schell (1991). There they argue that stigmatisation, or attachment of negative identity, implies social exclusion, so a relationship between means-testing and stigmatisation would cause means-testing to detract from 'the integrative aim of social policy' (p. 192). Why means-testing should be related to stigmatisation of beneficiaries has been attributed to various inherent discrediting elements – failure in self-sufficiency, association with undesirable reference groups and lack of power (see Deacon and Bradshaw, 1983). In addition, the base on which the use of means-tested benefits can be morally justified – that of citizenship – is relatively weak, in comparison with the more concrete principle of reciprocity underlying many contributory benefits (van Oorschot and Schell, 1991). However, Harris (forthcoming) has questioned the historical basis of this construction. In a non-European context, the relationship between stigma and means-testing may well be different. Saunders (1990) suggests that stigma may be less of a problem in take-up of benefits in Australia, where targeting is a structural component of most benefits.

Deacon and Bradshaw (1983) considered that, despite the attention paid to theoretical perspectives which contribute to an understanding of the meaning of stigma, the concept remained difficult to investigate empirically. They suggested that as time passed, with greater distance from the hated pre-war means-test, and greater familiarity with the modern form, the importance of stigma might diminish. A recent study suggests, however, that the negative associations of declaring personal circumstances for financial assessment persist and have been transferred to younger people and new entrants to eligible populations. Interviews conducted with recently separated mothers by Leeming and Unell (1992) illustrate the stigma still attached to seeking financial help from the Benefits Agency.

Target groups that are negatively valued

The next structural feature of a benefit that tends to depress take-up, according to van Oorschot and Kolkhuis Tancke, is being targeted at groups in society which are the subject of negative valuations. Income support is the 'safety net' scheme, designed to provide financial support for the poorest people. There is evidence of some people's reluctance to join the 'poor', or to be identified with them (Davies and Ritchie, 1988). Targeting benefits at the 'sick and disabled' can contribute to non-take-up of disability benefits among those who want to emphasise their abilities and the positive aspects of their lives (Hedges and Thomas, 1994).

While this kind of effect is usually interpreted at the client level, in terms of feelings and perceptions of individual claimants, it is equally as appropriate to think of the outcome in association with features of benefit design. The high take-up of retirement pension, seen to be targeted at those who have made substantial contributions to society through their past work, can be contrasted with the much lower take-up among pensioners of income support, the benefit targeted at the very poor.

Supplements to other sources of income

Van Oorschot and Kolkhuis Tancke suggest that there is greater probability of non-take-up among benefits designed to supplement other sources of income. This may be supported by the extent to which small amounts of means-tested benefits go unclaimed by people whose main income comes from other sources. For example, small amounts of family credit, a benefit designed to supplement earnings, are less likely to be claimed than larger amounts (Marsh and McKay, 1993).

Although there is some uncertainty about the take-up rate of income support by pensioners, the estimated average left unclaimed is relatively small (£7.85 per week in 1989) and in many cases would have supplemented the contributory retirement pension (DSS, 1993b). This does not detract from the seriousness of non-take-up among pensioners, for some of whom the amount forgone may represent a significant proportion of net income.

Leaving the initiative to the claimant

The last structural feature van Oorschot and Kolkhuis Tancke considered likely to act towards depressing take-up was a design that left the initiative to start the claiming process entirely to the claimant. This effect is dramatically illustrated by results of take-up campaigns in the early 1980s, when DHSS staff 'took back the initiative', visiting hospitals and day centres to offer patients and attendees a full benefit assessment. Local DHSS officers visited Adult Training Centres in Strathclyde in one such project in 1983 (DHSS, 1984) with the aim of 'ensuring that each attendee was receiving full entitlement to both supplementary and contributory benefits'. Of a total of 5,344 people interviewed, 3,092 received increases in weekly supplementary benefit and 313 new claims were successful. Welfare rights campaigns have also been influential in increasing take-up by assuming some responsibility for initiating the claiming process, described later in Chapter Five.

Taking in turn each structural feature in the schema proposed by van Oorschot and Kolkhuis Tancke, there does seem to be evidence to support its validity. Benefits which are associated with low take-up by eligible people, such as income support, housing benefit and family credit, have several and sometimes all the structural features identified. Benefits which are associated with full take-up show few of these features. For example, for most people the eligibility criteria and rules for child benefit are few and simple; it is non-means-tested, and not targeted at a negatively valued group. This benefit does supplement parents' other sources of income, of course, and the parent does have to take the initiative in making an application, showing how structural features alone do not explain high take-up. Factors acting at the administrative and client level are also important. The benefit is well known and eligibility criteria usually easily understood. The overall value of the benefit over 16 years of childhood is a substantial return for a single application. The appropriate time for application and the procedure is easily identified within the general arrangements that accompany the birth of a new baby. There is a complex interaction between factors at all three levels. In this chapter, however, the focus is on structural features of benefits.

So far we have considered only structural features identified by van Oorschot and Kolkhuis Tancke. Reviewing the British research literature suggests that there may be additional structural features that tend to contribute to low take-up by eligible people. Non-take-up seems likely to be enhanced in schemes that:

- include a test of disability
- overlap or interact with other benefits
- challenge cultural norms or characteristics.

Test of disability

Low take-up of non-means-tested disability benefits such as attendance allowance, mobility allowance and the previous non-contributory invalidity pension was demonstrated throughout the 1980s in local studies designed to investigate and improve use of benefits by people with disabilities (Phillips and Glendinning, 1981; Cohen and Tarpey, 1982; Cohen, 1983; Davis, 1984; Day, 1985). The medical examinations necessary for determination of entitlement to these benefits were so much disliked that Sumpton (1985) suggested that these had a similar effect in depressing take-up as a financial means-test. He found that the experience of mentally handicapped applicants and their carers was that such benefits 'do require a means-test – one of psychological and physiological nature' (p. 6).

Recent qualitative work has demonstrated again the deterrent effect of the medical examination. This often seemed the focal point of the claiming process, and could cause anxiety, apprehension and pain (Costigan *et al.*, 1992). The journey involved could cause problems in some cases, and the test provoked special anxieties among parents of children with disabilities. Hedges and Thomas (1994) found similar attitudes and experiences. The unsuitability of the medical examinations for people with variable conditions or remissions was frustrating, and the necessity for separate medicals for each separate benefit caused annoyance. In 1992, self-assessment of medical conditions was introduced in the new disability living allowance, attendance allowance and disability working allowance, in an attempt to eliminate some of the problems caused by examinations by medical staff.

In terms of this discussion, the move to self-assessment might be considered as the structural adjustment to improve take-up. Early results (Hedges and Thomas, 1994) suggest that people still have anxieties about this process. They worry about giving wrong answers, dislike having to emphasise the negative aspects of their lives and their problems, and find some of the questions ambiguous – especially explaining their 'need for help' (a complex concept). This early evidence suggests that tests of incapacity *per se* may still act towards depressing take-up despite efforts to reduce their intrusiveness.

Benefits which meet the additional financial needs of disabled people and those with long-term health needs now form a significant component of overall social security provision. If the suggestion made above, that a test of disability or incapacity is a structural feature that may act towards depressing take-up of a benefit, then there are interesting policy implications.

First, there is room for a debate about how far intervention at the administrative level to promote take-up of disability benefit can counteract the structural effects depressing take-up. Linked to this, there is the issue of how responsibility is shared for promotion of disability benefits.

Secondly, there is a need to consider whether sharpening or fine-tuning a test of disability or incapacity as a means of more precise structural targeting of a benefit would be associated with depression of take-up. It has proved hard to maintain levels of take-up of two benefits with precise and extremely sensitive financial tests, family credit and its predecessor family income supplement, in part due to the information and procedural requirements of operationalising the test (Boden and Corden, 1994).

Overlap and interaction

Benefits interact in various ways within the overall social security system. Chapter Five explains how some administrative procedural links such as 'passporting' can act towards increasing take-up. Here the concern is a different aspect of interaction, overlap in the criteria for eligibility. For example, one benefit may count as income in assessment for another. Thus, family credit is taken into account as income for purposes of assessment for housing benefit, and the net value is reduced.

There are complex household income consequences of overlapping benefits regulations in the population eligible for invalid care allowance (McLaughlin, 1991). The existence of such interactions is a potential force towards lowering take-up, because there is an inbuilt possibility that people make a wrong choice, leading to a combination that leads to underclaiming. It is often not easy to work out which combination is in the claimant's overall financial interest (NCC, 1983). Another example of benefit interaction is where receipt of one benefit is an essential criterion for eligibility for another. If entitlement to one benefit depends on receipt of another, as with severe disability premium in income support where entitlement depends, among other things, on receipt of attendance allowance or disability living allowance, lowered take-up of one benefit has an automatic 'knock on' effect on the second. These effects are structurally produced.

Effects at the client level of such structural features are well known. Overlaps and interactions are hard to understand. They make people puzzled and angry and contribute to misinformation and fear of jeopardising existing benefits by making additional claims (Hedges and Thomas, 1994). Experience of loss of entitlement to housing benefit after family credit is awarded can lead people to believe, wrongly, that it is an 'either/or' situation where people are not entitled to both benefits at once (Eardley, 1993).

Challenges to cultural norms

Earlier suggestions that eligible families may be deterred from applying for benefit if structural aspects challenge or conflict with normal budgeting patterns within the family (Deacon and Bradshaw, 1983) have been confirmed by later work. Women in two-parent families, who had responsibility for making the money go round and wanted to apply for family credit, were sometimes unable or reluctant to persuade working male partners to provide the necessary earnings information to demonstrate entitlement (Corden, 1991).

There is some evidence that the availability of benefits for carers conflicts with the cultural identity of relationships among some of the population entitled. Hedges and Thomas (1994) showed that identification with the term 'carer' was difficult for some parents of children with disabilities, or spouses. There is also evidence from some people in intimate relationships that receipt of financial payments in respect of the care they give seems inappropriate (Beresford, 1994).

There is also evidence that structural aspects of the benefits system conflict with cultural norms of some ethnic minority people. Low take-up among ethnic minority communities has been demonstrated in several local studies (Tarpey, 1984; Khera, 1984; Ritchie and England, 1985). A national survey of low-income families (NOP, 1990) found lower take-up of passported health benefits among family credit claimants from ethnic minorities. A national study of probation clients showed that black clients were less likely to apply for social fund crisis loans despite extensive financial problems (Stewart *et al.*, 1989). Various factors are likely to be contributing to this depressed take-up. Here we are concerned with the challenge to cultural norms of structural aspects of the benefit system. It is not considered a proper social role for orthodox Muslim women to deal with agencies outside their family (Cohen *et al.*, 1992). Gordon and Newnham (1985) describe the financial repercussions for a Muslim family income if daughters living at home do not sign on and receive benefits. Interviews conducted by Law *et al.* (1993) explain how, among young Bangladeshis and Pakistanis, reluctance to claim stemmed partly from cultural and community pressures and, particularly, from the perceived demands of Islam. Here, individual decision making leading to non-take-up can only be properly understood in the context of conflict between cultural norms and expectations, and the institutional and structural features of social security provision.

This section has found some evidence to support van Oorschot's thesis that there are structural aspects of benefits which tend to depress take-up. Their effect is indirect, in providing the context and parameters for administrative organisation and people's claiming behaviour. Nevertheless, they are important in understanding take-up. A number of particular structural features that appear to be working in this way have been discussed. It seems likely that there are others not identified here. It also seems possible that some of those structural features that depress take-up by eligible people also act to encourage applications from ineligible people. Family credit and disability working allowance are interesting in this respect – two benefits which have all the features identified by van

Oorschot and Kolkhuis Tancke as tending to depress take-up, as well as some of the additional features identified by this author. Both these benefits have high rates of applications from ineligible people. By January 1993 some 24,000 applications for disability working allowance had been received and some 2,000 people were receiving the benefit. So little research has been conducted on applications for benefits from ineligible people that it is not known how important structural features are. Certainly, complexity of the rules and apparent imprecision of eligibility criteria led to applications by ineligible applicants for family income supplement (Corden, 1987a).

The effect of time

Finally, before leaving aspects of structure and moving on to consider aspects of organisation and administration in the following chapters, consideration is given to the effect of time. There are important temporal aspects of benefit structure, although these have received little attention until recently, and do not appear in van Oorschot's schedule. The duration of awards has some bearing on the number and frequency of opportunities for joining or leaving different schemes, and has various implications that will affect take-up. Vincent *et al.* (1991) have recently addressed the importance of temporal aspects and suggest that attainable take-up rates can be expected to be lower for a benefit that has a relatively short duration of award but is targeted at a volatile population, such as income support, than for a benefit which, once awarded, lasts a relatively long time, such as child benefit. It is the structure of the benefit, and the way in which duration of award is linked with changing circumstances over time that is important here. In the case of financial support for children, one family unit may go in and out of eligibility for income support or family credit during the child-rearing years, with many opportunities for non-take-up (non-claiming, delayed claiming, erroneous awards). The same family unit, once it has claimed child benefit for each child, may experience a continuous award for 16 years in each case with little in the way of opportunity for non-take-up.

Other temporal aspects likely to be important include the length of time a scheme has been operating. Low take-up and high rates of applications from ineligible people are both features likely to be associated with new benefits. Traditionally, this has been considered at the client level in terms of assimilation of information. It is just as useful to focus on change at the structural level. A completely new benefit needs a new name, and it is inevitable that the choice of name will affect take-up. Early research on perceptions of the Department of Social Security literature following the 1988 re-organisation of social security (Hedges, 1988) showed that people associated the name 'family credit' with borrowing. Research three years later (Corden, 1992) showed belief that family credit would have to be repaid was still leading to non-take-up by eligible people. An initial proposal to call the most recently introduced income-related benefit 'disability credit' was abandoned because of the possible association with borrowing: we do not yet know what associations and perceptions are generally provoked by the name 'disability working allowance'. Hedges and Thomas (1994) suggest that any change in the benefits scheme causes problems and confusion in the short to medium term, automatically affecting take-up. Moreover, change can irritate people and may seem something to be viewed with suspicion, and such negative effects can take a long time to disappear. The effect of change may be especially important for first time claimants. A first time experience of claiming within a transitional structural situation, or when procedures and outcomes are different from those anticipated, may have more impact than the same experience for a person more used to changes within the scheme. This might act towards depressing take-up. On the other hand, a new entrant unaware that she was entering a new scheme or taking part in different procedures from those operating previously, might bring fewer erroneous preconceptions to the process, be more inclined to make enquiries and more receptive to information (Williams *et al.*, 1995).

At the time of writing, Walker was collating issues and examples that take account of time in poverty dynamics (Walker with Ashworth, 1994). He offers further perspectives on the dimension of time in targeting and administration of benefits.

This chapter has considered evidence from the British social security system within the framework of van Oorshot's schema of structural features that tend to depress take-up. It is hard to test the schema, and the effect of structural features remains largely theoretical at present. There is some supporting evidence from comparisons between benefits with different characteristics and different levels of take-up, and in studying what happens when there is reorganisation at the structural level or new benefits are introduced. Structural features comprise only one level of influence on take-up, however. The second tier of influence is administrative effect, the subject of the following three chapters.

Administrative effects: information

There is a considerable body of research conducted specifically to test or monitor administrative effects on take-up. Much of this research has been commissioned by the DHSS and the DSS as part of the commitment to evaluate benefits, and, recently, by the Benefits Agency in commitment to customer service. The Benefits Agency, established in 1991, is part of DSS, an Executive Agency set up under the Government's Next Steps Programme to manage the delivery of social security benefits (BA, 1994). Research on administrative effects has also been conducted for local authorities, and for voluntary organisations and consortia working in the interests of potential beneficiaries. Research by the National Audit Office to enquire into effectiveness, efficiency and economy in social security provision has included work of direct relevance to take-up issues. Research on administrative effects has included claimant surveys; discussions with people in target populations, with staff who administer benefits and with professional workers who get involved in the process; and observations in administrative offices. There are also studies based on statistical analysis.

The framework chosen for presentation of this research has moved away slightly from van Oorschot's second tier list of administrative factors increasing the probability of non-take-up. That included various aspects of communication, procedure, administration, interpretation and decision making. While these are essential features for consideration, there is some overlap in the specific elements as presented by van Oorschot and the second tier list lacks the sequential and chronological framework that is one of the strengths of both Walker's approach and that of Buckland and Dawson.

In this review, administrative effects on take-up are discussed under the following headings:

- information supply
- service provision
- application forms
- subsequent negotiations

- administrative links between benefits
- accuracy in decision making
- policing the system.

This chapter is concerned with information material.

Introduction

Looking back, in 1980, over 15 years of the Supplementary Benefit Commission, Briggs and Rees (1980) remarked on the striking change in the efforts and resources devoted to publicising the government's roles, objectives, policies and actions in the area of means-tested benefits. This development has continued, and the DSS/Benefits Agency now have a strong commitment to communication and information strategies. Information may be of critical importance to first time claimants.

Information about social security benefits is provided for the general public mainly in the form of leaflets and guides, which are made available through the post office network, and at local DSS and Benefits Agency offices and other key sites such as Job Centres, Health Centres, Information Bureaux and through professional workers. Promotion and advertising is conducted via the media. Additional access to information is offered through telephone helplines, discussed in the following chapter on service provision. This chapter focuses on informational literature and the media promotions.

At the client level, obtaining and understanding written and promotional material is afforded key importance in much of the literature on take-up (see Craig, 1991). Approaching this aspect from the perspective of design and distribution of informational material has been attempted less frequently, however. Research has been conducted on the effectiveness of DSS advertising, and the impact of different kinds of written information. There is also a recent stream of research which has investigated how to address the information needs of particular client groups and their advisers.

Formal advertising

The benefits that have received most attention in monitoring and evaluating the effects of formal advertising and benefit promotion are family credit and its predecessor, family income supplement (FIS). The early experience of the DHSS (Bolitho, 1976) was that continuous advertising of FIS was necessary in order to keep the number of recipients from falling. Monitoring experiments with different types of advertisements in the press, on television and local radio and by household leafleting, led the DHSS to the conclusion that television and press advertising, although expensive, was essential to maintain the recipient caseload. It was thought that the higher the advertising expenditure, the greater would be the likelihood of increasing the caseload. A subsequent statistical analysis (Atkinson with Champion, 1989) followed numbers of FIS recipients during 1971–80, taking into account changes in qualifying levels and changes in rules. No evidence was found that the formal advertising campaign had led to an appreciable increase in recipients.

Recently Ashworth and Walker (1992) have explored the changing characteristics of the family credit caseload, by longitudinal analysis of administrative records from April 1988 to December 1991. They found the effectiveness of the advertising campaigns varied, both in speed of impact and in the number of additional applications. The most successful advertising campaign in terms of additional applications was not reflected in the general caseload profile because of 'lags' and an unknown proportion of unsuccessful applications. There were 'no grounds to believe that the penetration of family credit is increasing among new applicants' (p. 11) and the authors suggested that if take-up of family credit is indeed rising (Fry and Stark, 1992; Marsh and McKay, 1993) we could expect the bulk of future applicants to come from the existing caseload.

An evaluation of the family credit campaign in spring 1989 by the Central Office of Information (COI, 1989) also found no firm evidence that the number of successful claims had increased, although a telephone survey suggested that overall levels of awareness and understanding of the eligibility criteria had been raised among the eligible population. In view of the expense of the FIS/family credit advertising campaigns (*Hansard*, 1980; Lynes, 1991) the possibility that it has no effect in increasing penetration of this benefit is challenging. Other ways of delivering more personalised information about the benefit, such as the message in child benefit books telling each family the level of income below which they qualify for family credit are cheaper and seem to be effective (Lynes, 1991). There may be a concentration effect here – the availability of the personalised information to people whose interest has been captured by general advertising.

What is missing from most studies of the effect of information delivery in advertising campaigns is any systematic analysis of applications from ineligible people. General advertising is known to have considerable effect in encouraging applications from people who do not qualify for benefit. Disability working allowance, introduced in April 1992, was publicised in an extensive media campaign. During the first month 92 per cent of claims which had been decided were rejected (Hansard, 1992). This level of rejection may have important repercussions on take-up. As mentioned earlier, research shows that previous experience of rejection or expectation of rejection acts to depress take-up by eligible people.

Some information is available about ways in which people have been misled by particular components of media advertising. As an example, qualitative research on reactions to the family credit advertising campaign (COI, 1989) demonstrated how misinformation could be imparted by visual images and messages in television and press advertisements. Much of the research done for the DSS advertising strategy tends to be small-scale qualitative work at the client level. If there is to be continued commitment to expensive advertising of particular benefits, there would seem also to be a need for some large-scale systematic research, that tests experiments in the advertising campaign (content, timing, frequency, outlet) against the experience of the target population (exposure, understanding, impact) and subsequent changes in the profile of all applications.

At any one time the DSS is using a number of personalised promotional strategies to increase take-up of individual benefits (the family credit message in the child benefit order book has been mentioned). In early 1982, a letter sent by the DSS to a quarter of a million people not apparently receiving one-parent benefit but whose child benefit books were issued in one name only was followed by about 8,000 new awards (Millar and Cooke, 1984). A useful line of enquiry might be to review all such initiatives, across the whole range of benefits, comparing the content of the message, the 'vehicle' for delivery and results of subsequent monitoring of effectiveness. A recent international postal survey about social security administration returned by 66 countries showed that targeted small-scale advertising was now the most favoured approach and thought to be most effective (Poirrier, 1993). One example was writing to people approaching retirement age to tell them in advance what their contributions record entitled them to and how to claim their entitlements. Newcastle Pension Directorate does send information to people approaching retirement age, encouraging them to make an application.

DSS literature

The take-up research reviewed by Craig (1991) provides considerable evidence of difficulties experienced or perceived by clients in respect of the literature provided by the DSS – leaflets, application forms and standard letters, and the effect in depressing take-up.

These are familiar themes, which have been confirmed in more recent work, for example the length and complexity of application forms (Boden and Corden, 1994); confusing or complicated language (MORI, 1990); unclear instructions and confusing layout (Costigan *et al.*, 1992); questions provoking feelings of intrusion or inquisition (Hedges and Thomas, 1994), and the enhanced effect for people with problems with literacy or writing (NACAB, 1991). There is less published research on broader supply-side issues at the administrative level, for example, how the design and distribution of written material affects application patterns, or the behaviour of advisers to claimants.

The main thrust towards improving literature came with the general scrutiny of administrative forms within government, leading to a White Paper in February 1982 (House of Commons, 1982). Following a commission from Salford Forms Market (later, the Plain English Campaign) to redesign eleven of the supplementary benefit forms and standard letters, an internal DHSS specialist forms unit was set up (Took, 1983b). Initial aims were higher professional standards and greater consistency in form production, and emphasis was laid on central control of new forms and the importance of testing. One of the unit's earliest jobs was to help the Open University develop a postal claim form for supplementary benefit (Took, 1983a).

The major social security changes in 1988 required a new generation of leaflets and forms, and the DSS embarked on a more structured communications strategy in their literature. A five tier hierarchy of information was introduced:

- overview leaflets providing introduction to social security
- promotional leaflets to client groups
- integrated leaflets and claim forms
- explanatory guides
- technical guides.

The overall aim was to make social security easier to understand and more accessible. Preliminary qualitative research on the first three levels of information investigated the reactions to the new material of different client groups and their advisers (Hedges, 1988). Using a 'client group' approach was usually approved, although often not spontaneously recognised as such. The new leaflets aimed at client groups generally worked quite well, although the social fund did not emerge as a coherent identity, and people found problems in achieving the calculations they wished to make for income support and family credit. Disadvantages identified included overlapping between client groups, problems of definition of target groups and self-identification of clients (particularly young people).

A new wave of qualitative research has accompanied the creation of the Benefits Agency and the introduction of new disability benefits. Results have queried the appropriateness of addressing the whole population of 'sick and disabled' people as a target group in promotional strategies. Discussions (Hedges and Thomas, 1994) showed that many people, properly within this group for purposes of social security, did not identify themselves here. They preferred to emphasise their abilities rather than what might appear inadequacies by joining this labelled group. Some people with particular health circumstances, for example mental illness, did not feel part of the 'sick and disabled'. The 'carer' terminology was not one which all 'carers' identified with. This is a complex issue, with differences in use and understanding of terminology by professionals and claimants. The researchers suggested that addressing the 'sick and disabled' in information strategies should be reassessed and group labels might be abolished altogether. Alternatively, narrower, more targeted descriptions might be sought, such as 'people with mobility problems'.

Leaflet design

Reviews of the literature on document design (Kempson, 1985; Rowlands, 1991) highlight the factors that make documents accessible to people with normal sight, including type size and weight, and the ways in which these are related to design features such as line length, interline- and word-spacing. The usefulness of ordinary printed informational material such as posters and leaflets may be reduced for people with visual impairment. Perkins (1991) points out that approximately 90 per cent of those with visual impairment are receiving some sort of benefit. Leaflets specially produced in large print or braille were considered helpful (Hedges and Thomas, 1994), but as with all DSS leaflets, problems existed in distribution and accessibility of updated versions.

The way that informational literature has been provided for people from ethnic minority backgrounds has been identified as one of the factors depressing take-up among this group (NACAB, 1991; NAO, 1991b; Cohen *et al.*, 1992). Most informational leaflets are available only in English. The leaflet *Which Benefit* is prepared in seven minority languages, and distributed to local offices, but the translation and presentation has been subject to some criticism (NACAB, 1991; Bloch, 1992). Bloch suggests that for some groups of people with low levels of literacy in a first language (especially Punjabi and Bengali speakers) translated leaflets are of limited value.

Informational literature may also have limited impact on English speakers with low literacy skills. Hedges and Thomas (1994) have identified people with learning difficulties as a group who need special promotional material to empower them to claim benefits independently.

Distribution of material

The hard task involved in distribution and maintaining accessible and attractive displays of up-to-date DSS literature has been recognised for a long time (Briggs and Rees, 1980; Graham, 1984). Some parents were still reporting in 1991 that the leaflets and claim forms they needed were difficult to find or obtain in person from DSS branch offices (Leeming and Unell, 1992). Similarly, advice agencies were reporting problems in distribution of benefit materials, such as delays in providing updated material or insufficient supplies (Hedges and Thomas, 1994; Perkins *et al.*, 1992). Gregory (1993), a benefits adviser relying on the mailing list service from the Stanmore leaflet distribution centre, questions the efficiency of the benefits material distribution service.

There appears to be no published research, on the supply side, of DSS distribution of literature and effects on take-up. Many studies at the client level provide detailed information about where people get their leaflets (for example, Costigan *et al.*, 1992). What is lacking is large-scale systematic research on the coverage and efficiency of the distribution scheme. It is not known whether the sources of leaflets reported by claimants represent their choice of supply, activity by professionals, or factors within the distribution scheme itself. It would be useful to know how distribution matches the number and pattern of applications, and what the 'turnover' rate is for different kinds of information about different benefits, in a variety of outlets.

In addition to providing written material, in 1992 information officers were appointed at local Benefits Agency offices to inform the public about social security benefits, identifying local customer needs and providing an appropriate service (NAO, 1993). Such initiatives can be effective in raising levels of understanding about benefits, as demonstrated by Bloch (1992) in interviews with people from a local Chinese community, where a 'benefit surgery' was staffed by Benefits Agency personnel in a Chinese community centre. Efforts to increase the take-up of social fund community care grants by local office information officers or social fund officers had variable success (Walker *et al.*, 1992). While one local office reported an intensive campaign to increase take-up among elderly people as 'expensive but effective', another 'failed to identify a substantial volume of unmet need' (p. 10).

This first chapter looked at administrative effects on take-up and focused on the official information and publicity material supplied by the DSS and the Benefits Agency. There has been a major commitment of resources in this area during the past decade. The budget allocated by DSS for expenditure on paid publicity activity stood at £7 million for 1993-94, with an additional £3.5 million for publicity work carried out by Agencies (DSS, 1994a). Major developments in design and presentation of material, and methods and scale of information-giving, have been accompanied by a commitment to research. There is a strong body of knowledge about the effects of informational aspects at the client level – the claimants' experience of access to information, and their understanding and utilisation. Of course, it is the client level effects that directly influence take-up, but it is at the administrative level that the information material is designed and distributed. What this chapter has shown is the relative paucity of systematic research concentrating on the supply side of information design and distribution. It is hard to find well-developed theoretical bases for the approaches taken in provision of information, and there are relatively few examples where the result of tests and experiments are readily accessible for discussion.

The supply of information is, of course, an area on which many local take-up campaigns have concentrated – distributing DSS material as well as literature designed independently. The effectiveness of take-up campaigns is discussed later, in Chapter Five. Here the focus has been on material designed and promoted by 'the system' itself. Information is provided in a number of ways, of course, and the following chapter considers other aspects of service provision in the administration of social security.

Administrative effects: aspects of service provision

This chapter is concerned with aspects of service provision that involve direct contact between administrators and the public.

For most people the main point of direct contact with social security administrators is the local Benefits Agency office, which offers general advice and information about the main benefits, and deals with applications for a range of contributory and non-contributory benefits. Claimants also make direct contact with Benefits Directorate offices at Newcastle and Fylde, mainly by telephone and letter, and some claimants have contact with District offices, or medical assessment centres. Every facet of communication between a claimant and the administrative system is a potential source of encouragement or constraint in the take-up process. There may be enhanced effects for people claiming for the first time.

While the Benefits Agency sees direct provision of advice and information about benefits as a main role, research shows that there is considerable distance between this image and claimants' perceptions. People claiming allowances and pensions for disability saw DSS (whichever locus of administration) primarily as an agency for assessment rather than an agency for providing advice or information (Costigan *et al.*, 1992). Indeed, some expressed a general reluctance to approach the DSS for advice, due to apparent inaccessibility of appropriate help; an expectation that the DSS, being the keeper of the public purse, would be more interested in deterring than facilitating claims; and a fear of instant assessment. A similar finding is that pensioners, a group which has traditionally expressed highest degrees of satisfaction with overall service from the DSS (Briggs and Rees, 1980; Victor, 1985; Austin *et al.*, 1994) thought DSS advice services were unlikely to be an important method of promoting take-up (Victor, 1985). Ethnic minority families were more likely than white families to get advice and help about income support outside DSS (MORI, 1990). If the image of the DSS as a source of help and advice is not shared by the claimant population, the effect on take-up of efforts to increase or improve this side of DSS activity is likely to be muted, or at least subject to a time-lag until the public image changes.

Locus of administrative office

For those claimants who do consider making personal contact with administrators, the locus of the appropriate office has important effects. The geographical dispersion of administration between central and local offices is often not understood by claimants. Indeed, the apparent fragmentation of responsibility contributed to the perceptions of some people with disabilities that the Benefits Agency appears to be, in certain ways, disorganised and incompetent (Hedges and Thomas, 1994). Being 'passed around' from office to office is disliked and has deterrent effects (Costigan *et al.*, 1992) – a finding with important implications for the 'one-stop shop' proposals (BA, 1992; Adler and Sainsbury, 1993).

Geographical access to local offices affects people's ability or inclination to visit. An interesting study in the rural US state of North Carolina in 1974, one of the few early economic studies to consider directly supply variables, used geographical distance from the nearest benefit office as a proxy for information available (Strauss, 1977). A policy conclusion was that take-up (enrolment in a new programme of cash assistance to blind, elderly and disabled people) was affected by the location of welfare offices and the medical assessment teams.

There is considerable evidence from client studies that the time, difficulty or cost of getting to a local office deter people from making the journey. Problems were specially reported by claimants in rural and industrial areas (NCC, 1983); people applying in person for supplementary benefit (Briggs and Rees, 1980); people with mobility problems (Hedges and Thomas, 1994); and lone parents who had to travel with children (Leeming and Unell, 1992). A survey of Citizens Advice Bureaux clients (NACAB, 1990a) showed that the cost of bus fares to a local office to apply for a crisis loan had put people off applying to the social fund.

Access into benefits offices may present problems to disabled people (Costigan *et al.*, 1992). Once inside the office, design features can have important effects on the claimants' experiences. The layout of Benefits Agency offices set obstacles in the process of claiming by lone parents since buildings were ill adapted to the needs of mothers with children (Leeming and Unell, 1992). They mentioned the stairs, lack of changing and feeding facilities, or refreshment facilities for children.

The Benefits Agency seeks detailed information about customers' experience and satisfaction with the physical environment, for example signposting, seating, toilet facilities and temperature (Austin *et al.*, 1994). In this survey, toilet facilities and facilities for children emerge as less important than quality of staff and privacy. However, the people interviewed in the survey had all visited their social security office in the last 12 months. The survey gives no measure of the extent to which potential claimants had been deterred altogether from going to the office.

The layout and facilities of the office are likely to be aspects of key importance for disabled people. Apparently minor factors such as the distribution of light can have a major impact on people with visual impairment. Perkins (1991) suggests that 'illumination, in combination with the signposting and other visual aids can do much to reduce a partially sighted person's reluctance to visiting public places' (p. 9).

There is evidence from a number of studies that, at the client level, much of the dislike of visiting local offices arises from being associated with other people with negative images (for example, see Corden, 1983; Leeming and Unell, 1992; Huby and Dix, 1992). The psychological effects of having to be in an office or waiting room with other 'undesirable' claimants are modified by two aspects of administration – delays in dealing with callers at the office, and the privacy available. The delay involved is particularly disliked, and identified as a deterrent to visiting offices in search of information or to make applications for benefits (Corden, 1983; Leeming and Unell, 1992; Costigan *et al.*, 1992). Lack of privacy has also been repeatedly identified by claimants in a number of studies as a deterrent to negotiations in a local office (Briggs and Rees, 1980; Hedges and Thomas, 1994). Customer surveys show that being dealt with privately is one of the most important aspects of service provision (Austin *et al.*, 1994) and all local offices, in the last few years, have made or improved provision for private interviews.

Quality of staff

The quality of staff is the other most important aspect of service provision at social security offices as identified by customer surveys (Austin *et al.*, 1994). There are issues of staff competence, and the accuracy and breadth of their knowledge, as well as their social skills in dealing with people. The ability of front line staff to give appropriate information to enable people to identify their eligibility and make an application will have a direct effect on take-up. The complexity of the benefit system is such that most staff will never attain full knowledge about all benefits. The aim of the Benefits Agency therefore is that when staff cannot provide information themselves, they can refer claimants on to the appropriate office with addresses or telephone numbers. In some cases this may act towards increasing take-up, but every additional new point of contact introduced into the process has its own range of factors, at both the administrative and the client level, that can also act towards depressing take-up. There are implications for the proposed introduction of the 'one-stop' service. The quality of the staff, and the efficiency and effectiveness of the referrals and links will be critical determinants of the overall effects on take-up.

A frequent research finding is that people often hope and indeed expect that one part of the social security system will lead to another, and if they ask about some entitlements they will automatically be told about others (Ritchie and Matthews, 1982). This tends to inhibit enquiries about other entitlements they might have. When people do press for a fuller analysis of their overall benefit situation, and get a confusing or inaccurate response, this can not only lead to non-take-up of current entitlements. It also makes people frustrated and annoyed and has a deterrent effect on future negotiations or advice seeking (Leeming and Unell, 1992). In research conducted for the advertising strategy development for family credit, people in the target population criticised some DSS local office staff for their lack of knowledge about family credit and their failure to suggest this benefit when people enquired about other low income benefits (COI, 1990).

On the other hand, adopting a comprehensive approach does not always have a positive effect on take-up. Leeming and Unell's study suggested that when lone parents received a 'package' of forms from the Benefits Agency, including forms for income support, family credit and one-parent benefit, their raised expectations could lead to disappointments and increase confusion. Moreover, being wasteful of documentation and the time of both staff and claimant, it could contribute to negative images of social security administration, which we know have deterrent effects on future take-up.

As would be expected, research shows that claimants have variable experiences in the ways they are treated by social security staff. While some lone parents felt that they were treated with the utmost tact and sympathy in the local office (Leeming and Unell, 1992), others thought that staff had been impersonal and confrontational. There is a tendency, across a number of benefits, for pensioners to report more positive feelings than other client groups in this respect (for example, Victor, 1985; Austin *et al.*, 1994). Negative feelings, on the other hand, tend to be reported more frequently by younger people with no children (Huby and Dix, 1992). In interviews with people of working age claiming low income benefits conducted by Dean and Taylor Gooby (1992), two-thirds said the way they had been treated or the attitude or inefficiency of personnel had led to their feeling some anger or annoyance.

Studies in the 1980s that addressed directly the way in which local DHSS office personnel dealt with claimants confirmed that among the range of attitudes of staff there was a degree of discrimination and prejudice. Beltram's interviews with staff and managers in local offices, and his discussions with claimants' representatives (1984), provided him with numerous indications of discrimination against certain types of claimants. His observations of local office practice and those of Howe (1985) showed the extent to which local office staff failed to provide advice and information to claimants, and how beliefs about claimants influenced the way they treated people, and could affect the outcome of enquiries and applications. Distinctions between the 'deserving' and 'undeserving' were frequently made, and these categories were attached not only to groups of clients (pensioners, for example, are often viewed sympathetically) but also to individuals. Cooper (1985) found that 'undeserving' claimants, suspected of cheating in some way or trying to claim supplementary benefit single payments too often, were refused new applications for single payments, although they had demonstrated need for a grant. People with certain kinds of mental illness and mental handicap may face discriminatory attitudes of a different sort. Hardie and Miller (1985) noted the anxieties and suspicion among some benefits staff when dealing with psychiatric patients.

Human prejudice has to be faced as an ineradicable feature (Beltram, 1984). It is likely to have greatest influence in discretionary schemes, and social security staff acknowledge the reality of its effect. Officers administering the discretionary social fund were sensitive to the possibility that their decisions would be clouded by prejudice (Walker *et al.*, 1992). They realised that their own personal circumstances affected attitudes to different claimants, and would influence whether applications resulted in awards or refusals.

Several studies have demonstrated the key role in encouraging or preventing take-up that a receptionist can play by effectively rationing access to information or other staff (Briggs and Rees, 1980; Hedges and Thomas, 1994). There is evidence from social fund monitoring projects (Smith, 1990) and research studies (Walker *et al.*, 1992) that applications to the social fund may be discouraged or dissuaded at the reception desk.

An additional factor for black people or people from ethnic minorities is the possibility of meeting racist attitudes among staff in social security offices. Beltram's series of interviews following the 1980 reform of supplementary benefit led him to the conclusion that some DHSS staff lacked understanding of the problems of ethnic minorities (1984, p. 99). Observations in local offices conducted during the same period by the Policy Studies Institute demonstrated that racial prejudices common in society at large were reflected by the staff (Berthoud, 1984; also reported in Gordon and Newnham, 1985). More recently, interviews with people from ethnic minority families show that some people believe they have experienced racist attitudes from staff (Cohen *et al.*, 1992; Bloch, 1992). In a study of provision of social security benefits to black minority ethnic communities (Law *et al.*, 1993) African-Caribbean lone parents were particularly critical of their treatment by Benefits Agency staff.

A study of probation clients (Stewart *et al.*, 1989) showed that black clients were less likely than white people to apply for social fund crisis loans despite extensive financial problems, and suggested that this was likely to be due to discriminatory attitudes of counter staff. Becker and Silburn (1990), however, in a national study of families taking financial or social fund problems to social workers, concluded that 'in general, there is little, if any evidence of differential treatment along ethnic or racial lines by social fund officers or social workers' (p. 56). A report of the experiences of local Citizens Advice Bureaux in helping ethnic minority families with social security issues showed that some local bureaux had found the views of members of Medical Appeal and Social Security Appeal Tribunals towards minority claimants to be negative or racist (NACAB, 1991). The NACAB study confirmed that low take-up was a characteristic of ethnic minority communities, and argued that the risks of racism affecting take-up are higher in discretionary schemes.

Leaving aside aspects of prejudice, communication between people from ethnic minorities and local office staff may be difficult anyway, if staff do not share the claimant's language (Gordon and Newnham, 1985; NACAB, 1991; Amin with Oppenheim, 1992; Cohen *et al.*, 1992). The approach in many local offices has been to rely on informal interpreting from family or friends or voluntary organisations, or the goodwill of staff with shared languages. There has been some criticism of this approach. If staff rely on informal interpreting they are likely to acquire some inaccurate information which will affect take-up (NACAB, 1991). Using friends, relatives or staff who are not trained interpreters could have adverse consequences for both claimants and the Benefits Agency (Bloch, 1992). The discussion cannot be monitored properly and the interpreter retains control. This creates conflict for adjudication staff, and may make it difficult to investigate fraudulent claims. Bloch (1992) confirmed the need for professional interpreters to reduce the language barrier faced by ethnic families in local offices when they try to get local staff to understand what they want.

It is not only ethnic minority families who face barriers in communication with administrators. Hedges and Thomas (1994) drew attention to communication problems faced by people with impaired sight, hearing or speech difficulties if staff with appropriate experience or skills were not available.

One further aspect that may affect communication is the gender relationship between staff and claimants. Research has not yet addressed this directly, but there are some indications that it should be considered. For religious and cultural reasons it may be inappropriate for some Asian women to discuss personal issues with a male member of staff if they come to the local office (Bloch, 1992). Such discussions with men may be difficult for some non-minority women as well. Leeming and Unell's discussions with lone mothers (1992) led them to suggest that women who have experienced relationship breakdown may prefer to deal with female staff.

Telephone communication

Telephone communication with the DSS/Benefits Agency provides additional contact for making enquiries, supplying information, responding to the DSS in support of applications, checking progress of applications or querying results. The Department's own customer surveys indicate an increase in the use of telephone communications and there has been considerable recent investment in technology and networks. Sainsbury *et al.* (1993) have questioned how far this increased use represents preference. Customer surveys show that the main improvements sought by people using the telephone to conduct business with the DSS/Benefits Agency are to be put straight through, not to be kept hanging on, to have more lines available, and for staff to call them back when appropriate.

Independent research shows that experiences of telephoning local Benefits Agency offices or the remote processing offices are still highly variable (for example, Boden and Corden, 1994; Costigan *et al.*, 1992). While some people get through quickly to the appropriate person, with satisfactory outcome, others report jammed switchboards, or unhelpful responses. Research with lone parents (Leeming and Unell, 1992) led those authors to suggest that experience of being 'passed round' to staff, delays and expense act towards depressing take-up. The cost of long-distance telephone calls to Fylde can be inhibiting (Corden, 1987a; Hedges and Thomas, 1994).

Recent developments in specialised telephone advice lines are still being evaluated, but there are some early indications of claimants' experiences. Interviews with people with disabilities (Hedges and Thomas, 1994) showed low levels of awareness of the disablement information advice lines run by the DSS and DIAL (an umbrella organisation) and the FREELINE and BEL helpline. The concept of offering help with partial completion of forms (the BEL facility) was viewed positively by claimants. However, the experience of some advice agencies who had used BEL was that the system was overloaded, gave inaccurate information, and the use of 'phone back' techniques was unpopular with claimants. The experience of some Age Concern groups was that claims made with assistance through the BA helpline were less likely to be successful – staff apparently had insufficient training and time available to ensure that an application accurately reflected the disabled person's needs (Age Concern, 1992a).

One message from these early results is that although extending telephone facilities offers new opportunities to encourage take-up, at the same time there are possibilities of introducing additional deterrent effects. Very high standards of service delivery will be necessary to match the expectations raised and prevent frustrations and disappointment, which we know have deterrent effects.

Early responses to promotional material supplied in audio and video tapes seem enthusiastic (Hedges and Thomas, 1994). It is important to set this in the context of video ownership. *Social Trends* (1994) shows that while 72 per cent of all heads of households possessed a video cassette recorder in 1992, this fell to only 48 per cent of the economically inactive (Table 6.7). Availability of audio and video material for claimants sets new challenges for distribution and delivery; and a need for thorough evaluation of the balance between the cost and any subsequent increase in take-up. The early results provide further evidence of how any new opportunity to encourage take-up automatically creates new possibilities of negative experiences as well: for example, people without videos were annoyed that they did not have access to the early morning information programmes about disability benefits (Hedges and Thomas, 1994).

Advice and information from outside DSS

Claimant surveys and studies of the claiming process provide abundant evidence that much of the information and advice that affects take-up comes from sources other than the DSS. People who are influential include those in respondents' informal networks – relatives, friends, neighbours or colleagues at work, as well as staff in specialist agencies such as Citizens Advice Bureaux, and professionals working within health, housing, social services and education. There is considerable transfer of information and help from independent and voluntary organisations working in the interests of special groups. Ritchie and Matthews (1982) suggest that the strength of influence of other people in encouraging claims comes from the authority in which such people are held, and the legitimacy and acceptability of claiming that they bestow. Recent interviews with lone parents (Leeming and Unell, 1992) stress the role of intermediate agencies in directing people to entitlement, encouraging contact with the DSS, providing a second opinion on DSS information or decisions, and mediating in cases of difficulty.

Evidence for the effectiveness of advice from intermediate agencies also comes from the extensive literature covering local take-up campaigns and independent initiatives to promote benefits. This has been comprehensively reviewed already (Falkingham, 1985; Alcock and Shepherd, 1987). For the purposes of this paper, which focuses on 'supply side' issues, it is useful to consider the relationship between the DSS/Benefits Agency and those agencies which provide information that influences take-up. Little direct research attention has been paid to this essential relationship, which may be a fruitful area for further work.

The DSS has always acknowledged the important effect of independent advisers, but systematic efforts to enhance and support this role have been rather late in emerging. Independent advisers were recognised as a group requiring specialist literature in the new communication strategy accompanying the 1988 benefit reorganisation. Preliminary qualitative work indicated some people's preference for sources of briefing and reference material other than the DHSS (Hedges, 1988). The DSS/Benefits Agency are now actively pursuing the information needs of independent benefits advisers (Perkins *et al.*, 1992; Hedges and Thomas, 1994). Recent discussions with disabled people (Costigan *et al.*, 1992) and people from ethnic minorities (Bloch, 1992) have re-emphasised the potential importance of professional health workers and community groups, for example, in influencing take-up in groups where non-take-up is known to be a problem.

Giving advice and information about social security can be a delicate issue for some professional workers, however, and the activities of independent advisers can, in turn, present powerful challenges to DSS administrative procedures. Relationships have covered a wide spectrum between confrontation and partnership.

Conflicts for independent advisers between the policy aims of benefits and the possible outcomes for their own clients can constrain their potential power in influencing take-up. An example was the opposition to family income supplement among some trade unionists who might have been in a position to promote the benefit, because of the link they saw with the maintenance of low wages by employers. Advisers and professionals in touch with disabled people have emphasised the professional conflicts they face in the emphasis on inability and dependency that is necessary in applying for disability benefits (Sumpton, 1985). Social workers in touch with families on income support have been reluctant to encourage applications for social fund budgeting loans when repayments will depress weekly incomes (Becker and Silburn, 1991). Stewart and Stewart's study of the use of the social fund by clients of social services departments (1991) detected an agency effect on the pattern of applications, as a result of social workers' reluctance to advise people to apply for loans. While 80 per cent of clients in regular contact with social workers applied for a social fund grant, most applications for budgeting loans were made before advice was sought from a social worker, or when a claimant was advised only by DHSS staff. Craig (1990) describes the conflicts faced by independent advice centre staff with the implementation of the social fund. How far successful applications to the social fund were affected by policies of non-cooperation or determined advocacy is hard to assess.

Conflicts of time and priorities of work for independent advisers who are in a position to influence take-up (Perkins *et al.*, 1992) are also an issue. The place of welfare rights work in social work administration, for example, has been closely examined (Stewart, 1989). There are similar dilemmas for specialist advice agencies (Hedges and Thomas, 1994). How far should they respond to increased demands for information about benefits that are to some extent produced by DSS promotions, when their own resources are constrained, and overload results in non-responsiveness?

On the other hand, energetic lobbying or campaigning by the independent sector, which can have dramatic effects on take-up, can produce conflict and administrative disruption for the DSS, as illustrated for example by the Strathclyde postcard campaign (Oliver and Melling, 1980). It was partly to avoid further such disruptions and to regain control of benefit promotion that the DSS embarked on some local initiatives with independent agencies that came close to a partnership model. In terms of increasing take-up, there were dramatic successes. Staff from local benefit offices and Strathclyde Welfare Rights visited adult training centres in Strathclyde and assessed the needs of disabled trainees. A total of 5,344 people were interviewed, of whom 3,092 received increased weekly supplementary benefit. There were also 313 successful new claims, as well as new and increased awards of attendance and mobility allowance and non-contributory invalidity pension (DHSS, 1984). A similar exercise was conducted in Birmingham by local officers seconded to Birmingham Social Services Department, who discovered that 74 per cent of trainees in four adult training centres were not receiving full benefit entitlement (Day, 1985).

The fact that this type of screening by staff able to authorise benefit payments could be so effective was partly associated with the structure of supplementary benefit at that time, incorporating a range of additional payments on top of standard entitlements. The number of permutations possible increased the chance of not receiving a full entitlement of supplementary benefit. Income support has a simpler structure and fewer separate payment components. Alongside changes in benefit structures, and developments in administrative procedure and technological innovations, go corresponding developments in relationships and levels of communication between the DSS/Benefits Agency and independent advisers. Whether the new flexibility in service provision at a local level will spawn a new generation of effective local partnership initiatives to increase take-up remains to be seen.

Information technology

Developments in computer technology have introduced new opportunities for providing advice about social security, and opportunities for potential claimants and their advisers to test eligibility for a range of benefits. The earliest computer experiment (Adler and du Feu, 1975) produced disappointing results. People were invited to call at an information centre where clerical staff used a computer to assess eligibility and 'best buys'. Feasibility was demonstrated, but few people took advantage of the opportunity, and even fewer appeared to take action as a result.

There were a number of subsequent attempts to develop computer-based welfare benefits information systems, reviewed by Dawson *et al.* (1990). The main problems in a programme developed for use by Citizens Advice Bureaux advisers (Otley and Kempson, 1982) were reluctance of staff to spend the time required with individual clients, and the expense of updating the programme. Opportunities for using computers to give welfare rights advice in the primary care field were spotted early by a London GP, who has conducted substantial developmental work in this area (Jarman, 1985).

The early initiatives were monitored by the DHSS, who conducted their own experiment, locating machines in local offices for claimants' own use (Epstein, 1984). The machines appeared popular, and apparently successful. One month after installation half the users who had learned they were eligible are reported to have made a claim. The system was not extended as updating proved too expensive, but DHSS resources went into the Alvey Demonstration Project (Dawson *et al.*, 1990) – a research programme to investigate the general development of welfare benefit advice systems. In Northern Ireland a computer programme, developed by the Community Information Service for advisers to use in consultation with claimants, was demonstrated in a number of venues and appeared to be successful in increasing take-up (Alcorn and Smith, 1985). Advantages recognised in using computers included a more active role for the claimant, and the boost to confidence and knowledge.

From research in the Alvey project, Dawson *et al.* (1990) concluded that there was considerable potential for developing information technology for benefits for low-income households. Computer assistance could contribute to demystifying the claim process, and greater empowerment. There were considerable advantages in the speed at which machines could scan circumstances and provide information. Disadvantages were mainly associated with the impersonality, and inability of machines to counsel or give assistance.

The latest developments have been mainly in the field of hand-held computers. Bateman (1992) piloted computer-based welfare rights work in social services and concluded that in order to reach its potential, a computer strategy must be driven by end users, both in terms of hardware and software. The investment in training time needed for staff to get maximum value from the technology could be substantial. Bateman evaluated the three hand-held 'packages' currently on the market (including the Lisson Grove programme which has been developed from Jarman's original work). These are known to be widely used by welfare rights advisers (and have found a separate place in research, for checking eligibility in survey work).

This chapter has reviewed the literature and research that throws light on the effect on take-up of some of the contacts between administrators and the public. There are numerous facets of interaction which may be influential, all of which may usefully be considered from the supply side as well as at the level of client experience.

At present, the formal application for benefit is made through the medium of an appropriately signed and dated application form. The following chapter considers what is known, from the supply side, about the forms and documents used in the administration of benefit. The chapter goes on to consider other procedural aspects, including administrative links between benefits.

Administrative effects: application procedures and outcomes

This chapter considers administrative negotiations and decision making that lead to awards and payments, or rejections, and includes discussion of administrative error.

Application forms

The application form has a key position in the claiming process, with legal status as a formal claim to entitlement by the claimant, at the same time as being the main means whereby the DSS collects information necessary to determine eligibility. In addition, the application form may be used by the DSS to supply particular points of information, or explain why information is necessary, in order to guide prospective claimants and increase accuracy and efficiency. Inevitably, there are tensions between the different needs of the users of the forms.

Research at the client level has repeatedly shown that the general deterrent effect of having to fill in a form is increased by length, complexity and poor design, and by problems or delay in obtaining a form. For example, problems with the income support application form reported by claimants with children included complexity, lack of space and use of complicated language (MORI, 1990). Elderly people visiting Age Concern offices for help with application forms demonstrated that problems included the complexity of design, the jargon in the language used, the lack of availability of up-to-date forms, and the fact that small print and coloured paper made forms hard to read (Age Concern, 1992b). Occupational therapists who helped clients deal with social security forms confirmed that the language used and the small print made forms inaccessible to some people (Perkins *et al.*, 1992). Impaired sight and limited physical dexterity or mobility can prevent some people altogether from dealing with forms (Costigan *et al.*, 1992; Hedges and Thomas, 1994).

The language used on some forms, even when not particularly complex, may not be interpreted as intended, causing people to answer questions in the wrong way and possibly exclude themselves from eligibility. For example, the concept of 'needing help' used on the form for disability living allowance caused some people to exclude themselves on the basis that a person who does not receive help does not need help (Hedges and Thomas, 1994). The layout and presentation give powerful messages that may encourage or deter. While the initial application form for family credit was generally approved by self-employed applicants, the comparison between this and the supplementary enquiry form they subsequently received suggested to some self-employed people that the amount of detail required and the complexity of the form represented a deliberate attempt at deterrence by the DSS (Boden and Corden, 1994). Noble *et al.* (1992) also found that forms for self-employed family credit applicants presented special problems.

The language, complexity and length of forms present special barriers to take-up among ethnic minority families (MORI, 1990; NOP, 1990; NACAB, 1991; NAO, 1991b; Cohen et al., 1992). Special attention to ethnic minority groups was paid when the postal claim form for unemployed supplementary benefit claimants was introduced in 1982 (Martin and Gigg, 1983). The internal monitoring and evaluation exercise detected no subsequent change in claiming patterns in the local offices studied. The authors' conclusion was that ethnic minority people resolved any difficulties with the postal form in the same way as they dealt with applications under the previous system – seeking help from children, friends or community representatives. It has been suggested that this type of dependence on informal translation may have adverse consequences for both claimants and the DSS/Benefits Agency, as previously discussed. In the case of the social fund application forms, where the onus lies on the applicant to provide whatever information is felt to be appropriate to support an application, a particular problem may face ethnic minority families (NACAB, 1990a).

The initiatives taken to improve application forms following the Rayner scrutiny (House of Commons, 1982), and the establishment of the specialist forms unit have already been described (p. 29). It was recognised that forms could represent a significant hurdle in claiming (Warder and England, 1981) and there has been a major commitment to improvement and development during the last decade. New forms are usually tested at the design stage, to help eliminate major problems in layout or language, but little of such work appears to have been published and generally disseminated. An exception is the recent study conducted during the design of the disability working allowance form (Silke, 1992). An experimental approach tested alternative questions to see how well a self-assessment form would work in practice, when people described how they were affected by disability. For example, a two per cent 'failure rate' in the prototype form was increased by the impact of excluding or replacing questions. However, the researchers observed that it was difficult to assess the extent to which such relatively low failure rates could be considered reasonable. Despite rigorous testing, the perfect form is unlikely to be achieved.

Once in operation, improvements in application forms are incorporated in subsequent editions on the basis of administrative experience, or the requirements of changes in the regulations. Again, there is little in the way of published material on the adequacy and quality of information supplied on application forms currently in use. The revised postal claim form for supplementary benefit (necessary after the full introduction of housing benefit in 1983) was evaluated internally (Gigg, 1983) in an exercise that considered answers to individual questions on a sample of applications. Improved design had reduced the number of forms that had to be returned for proper completion from 30.5 per cent to 18.5 per cent. Analysis of the reasons for return demonstrated the effect of form design on adequacy of information supplied in support of applications. For example, single claimants were leaving out whole sections because the first questions in those sections referred to children and they assumed the rest were irrelevant to their own circumstances. Further analysis of the content of information supplied by claimants on forms (adequacy, gaps, error, inappropriate material) in relation to the characteristics of claimants and the outcomes of the applications (awards, refusals, further enquiry) could provide useful indicators of effects on take-up of different layouts, language or instructions. Applications made by first time claimants may give particularly useful information in this respect, since they have not yet learned by experience how to cope with structural design imperfections, which application forms from experienced claimants may disguise.

Subsequent negotiations

Following receipt of an application form, a number of other negotiations or procedures may be necessary before a decision can be made about entitlement. Further information or clarification may be sought from the claimant. Supporting information or verifications may be sought from third parties such as employers. Information may be checked internally with other Benefits Agency records or the Contributions Agency. Links between social security and immigration policy may lead to checks with the Home Office (Amin with Oppenheim, 1992). A separate medical assessment may be a procedural requirement. It is not possible to review all possible permutations and outcomes across different benefits here. What is possible is to make general points, for which there is evidence in the literature.

First, every supplementary enquiry to the applicant has the potential to encourage or deter, with subsequent effect on take-up. Enquiries for clarification or further information, which are necessary for proper determination of eligibility, may be interpreted as challenges to truthfulness, or a demonstration of initial inadequacy in form-filling, with subsequent drop-out (Corden, 1987b). Graham (1984) showed that psychological barriers against applying that had been overcome in the initial application could easily re-establish themselves when income was queried. It is worth setting this finding in a numerical context, to demonstrate the potential deterrent effect of queries. Costigan *et al.* (1992) found that about one in ten of the participants in their study of the process of applying for disability benefits reported having an application form returned by DSS with queries, and one in ten had been asked for further information (with higher percentages in the case of invalid care allowance). One quarter of these communications from DSS caused some difficulty.

On the other hand, an experience that also causes particular difficulty is when silence follows an application (Costigan *et al.*, 1992; House of Commons, 1993). Letters of acknowledgement of applications, holding letters, or other indications of progress and timing of the administrative procedure help to remove uncertainty, are generally positively viewed and help to encourage participation.

The second general point to make is that procedural delay has a number of effects on take-up. There is evidence that a number of people lost benefit, or other services passported through entitlement, during the first year of disability living allowance as a direct result of administrative delay in adjudication (House of Commons, 1993). The implications of the losses incurred could be great; particularly harsh results included loss of access to the independent living fund, or the death of applicants before administration of special rules for terminally ill people.

Even if an award is eventually made following administrative delay, the effect of being without benefit during the waiting period can be harsh. Lone parents found that telephoning Benefits Agency branch offices did not help to bring applications to a conclusion. It was necessary to go in person 'to unlock the process' or get help from an advocate (Leeming and Unell, 1992). Cohen (1983) reports that the delay experienced by people with disabilities was interpreted as an indication that the DSS gave low priority to disability benefits, and reinforced ideas that disabled people are relatively unimportant. In addition, delay discouraged appeals or requests for review when eventual decisions were unfavourable – people could not bear the idea of any more red tape when they had waited so long already.

As well as these general deterrent effects, which may subsequently be projected across a range of benefits, being without benefit whilst eligible can lead to serious budgeting difficulties (Corden and Craig, 1991). Indeed, the experience of such financial problems while waiting for in-work benefits to be delivered following a move from unemployment can destroy their incentive effect in the next period of unemployment (Corden and Craig, 1991), and lead to families' reluctance to leave the income security of out-of-work benefits (McLaughlin *et al.*, 1989).

One interesting aspect of delay is the seasonal pattern that eventually develops in the numbers of applications processed, due to DSS staffing arrangements. Analysis of the family credit caseload statistics (Ashworth and Walker, 1992) shows a distinct seasonal patterning, with the number of applications processed in December only half of that in peak months in the summer and autumn, and a seasonal low in August. The researchers suggest that this pattern is driven by administrative considerations – Christmas means that December is a three working-week month, and the August low reflects staff summer holidays. It is known that the Christmas period and school summer holidays are especially difficult financially for low-income families, yet it is these months when the Benefits Agency offices are least well staffed to deal with applications.

There are numerous examples from individual benefits of delays that are procedurally induced. Boden and Corden (1994) explained how the construction of the application procedure for family credit almost inevitably meant that applications from self-employed people would take longer to process than those from employees. Eliciting information about earnings was consigned to a separate and distinct phase from that of the initial application for most self-employed people, automatically building in at least three or four additional days processing time. For some benefits long processing times are the norm. An enquiry by the National Audit Office (1992) demonstrated that half the first claims for war pensions in 1990–91 took more than 39 weeks to clear. One set of case papers could move up to 30 times between different administrative sectors, each movement representing one day in clearance time. This is an extreme example, but it illustrates clearly how some people are kept as eligible non-claimants by the administrative system itself. If claimants waiting a long time for decisions try telephoning, then time spent in locating casepapers prevents other people's access to the telephone lines and diverts administrative resources which could be spent on decision making.

There are also possible effects at the client level of this type of administrative delay. Claimants' frustration is easily projected onto experiences anticipated in trying to claim other entitlements, depressing, in turn, take-up of other benefits.

If third parties are involved in the application, then the administrative procedure may be automatically lengthened by the time taken to contact them and elicit a reply. Neither the DSS nor the applicant has direct control over third party response, and compliance cannot be guaranteed. Noble *et al.* (1992) and Marsh and McKay (1993) found little evidence of employers' non-co-operation in supplying evidence of earnings for family credit adjudication, or their collusion to manipulate earnings data to facilitate claiming by employees. Nevertheless, among family income supplement and family credit applications eventually rejected as a result of lack of sufficient supporting information, there have always been a number which have not progressed because employers do not reply to enquiries from the Family Credit Unit. Qualitative research with applicants for family income supplement (Corden, 1987b) illustrated how this was contributing to non-take-up. An enquiry by the National Audit Office to employers' organisations showed that while employers generally were able to supply information required by the Family Credit Unit, they resented the administrative time that this took (NAO, 1991b).

In addition, at the client level, the expectations that third parties may be drawn into the administrative procedure can deter applications (even when this assumption is incorrect). Thus, different claimant studies have demonstrated non-take-up of family income supplement in case the employer was involved, or an accountant had to be approached (Corden, 1987b); reluctance to apply for a rent allowance in case the administrative process alerted the landlord (Ritchie and Matthews, 1982); reluctance to apply for benefits in case that triggered attention from immigration authorities (Tarpey, 1984).

The connection between immigration status and entitlement to benefits can lead to an additional administrative procedure for some applicants – passport checking, or requirements for evidence of marriage or other relationships. Such procedures have been criticised on the grounds that they represent racial discrimination (Gordon and Newnham, 1985). The effect on take-up of including passports within whatever documentary evidence is required to support a claim is unclear. What is clear is that the practice is often resented and feared (Gordon and Newnham, 1985; Amin with Oppenheim, 1992).

A different kind of extension of administrative procedure occurs when the supporting evidence depends on results of a medical assessment. There are different kinds of medical assessments for different benefits, which cannot all be reviewed here. The medical assessments necessary for attendance allowance and mobility allowance received much criticism (for example, Buckle, 1988; NACAB, 1990b) and the general deterrent effect (Costigan *et al.*, 1992; Hedges and Thomas, 1994) has already been discussed, within the focus on the structure of benefits. The following section, considering the consistency and accuracy of decision making, has more to say about medical assessments.

In addition to those whose medical assessment takes place at home, a number of other claimants receive home visits. This area appears to have received little research attention, possibly associated with the general moves to postal application procedures, and redeployment of staff away from home visiting during the past decade. What recent evidence there is suggests that the moves away from home visiting may, in some cases, not be encouraging take-up among some groups of claimants. The results of a questionnaire sent to local groups of a major voluntary organisation working in the interests of elderly people, led to the conclusion that the home visiting service is essential for elderly people who have difficulty visiting a local office. In some areas there appeared to be considerable difficulty in arranging such visits (Age Concern, 1992b). The home visiting service from Disability Benefits Centres, to help people fill in application forms for disability benefits, appeared to vary widely in local areas, from evidence presented to the Social Security Committee (House of Commons, 1993).

Hinkley reviewed research on the delivery of general information and advice services to elderly people. The most acute needs were experienced by those over 75 years of age, the immobile and housebound and elderly people in rural areas. For some, home visits would be the only way of supplying proper information and advice (Hinkley, 1992).

While all communications between administrative staff and claimants are important and can affect take-up of current and future entitlements, the effect of a notice of rejection is known to have a particular impact. This is especially important in view of the large number of rejections generated by some of the current schemes, such as family credit and disability working allowance. About 50 per cent of first time applicants for family credit are refused. Replies from postal questionnaires targeted at potentially eligible populations in two local areas (Noble *et al.*, 1992) demonstrated that the actual experience of being refused was a deterrent to trying again. It was not just a dislike of being rejected; for some, the experience of rejection entrenched views of ineligibility that did not change when subsequent changes in family circumstances or benefit upratings converted ineligibility into eligibility. In a recent study of low-income families, Marsh and McKay (1993) showed that, controlling for other factors, significant numbers of eligible non-claimants of family credit remembered being rejected for either family credit or family income supplement. Of those who did eventually apply, 19 per cent were successful. The median time taken to re-apply was 35 weeks. These findings can be interpreted in several ways. One possibility is that they confirm people's dislike of a 'kick in the teeth', shown by earlier studies to be a powerful deterrent to take-up (Corden, 1987b), and suggest that it takes even those who are bold enough to re-apply some considerable time to expose themselves again to the possibility of failure. It is important to remember here that all negative experiences generated by the administrative system may be projected onto expectations of future claiming experiences across a range of means-tested and non-means-tested benefits. Noble *et al.* (1992) came to the conclusion that a significant proportion of non-take-up of family credit was explained by the administrative hurdles that had to be crossed, and the negative effects on claimants who failed at some stage while trying.

In concluding this section on negotiations with claimants, it is worth looking at the method of payment. A move to automatic credit transfer (ACT) and less frequent benefit payments proceeded more slowly than expected, for a number of reasons, partly due to customer preferences (NAO, 1985). The subject has recently been controversial, and the suggestion has been made that a reduction in the number of counter payments made by sub post offices would hasten the demise of the smaller offices. The method of payment has received little direct research attention. However, there is some evidence that there may be influences on take-up. The post office is known to be an important source of general information about benefits. The displays of posters and leaflets are known from a number of studies to be influential in maintaining levels of general awareness among the population, and to trigger applications. There may be fewer opportunities for exposure to advertising and leaflets if more people are drawn into ACT, or visit the post office to draw benefits less frequently.

Secondly, the availability of weekly cash benefit may have important budgeting implications for families. Recent studies of self-employed recipients of family credit (Corden, 1992; Eardley, 1993) have shown that people whose personal and business finances are closely intertwined, and those who have difficulty in access to finance from their banks because of large overdrafts, rely heavily on the regular availability of cash from the post office in their benefit income. At very low income levels, the difference between staying in work and returning to unemployment may depend on whether low earned incomes are manageable in terms of practical budgeting arrangements rather than on overall net incomes. It seems likely that some families might prefer the security of out-of-work incomes if weekly or monthly cash were not available through the post office.

In considering the impact of methods of payment on take-up, it is interesting to note recent awareness of how methods and frequency of payment affect the measure of take-up itself. Benefits that are paid four weekly in arrears automatically create the possibility that because they have not yet had any of their entitlement, some people who are technically in receipt identify themselves among those who are not receiving benefit when they take part in household surveys. Questionnaire schedules have to be sensitive to this if they are to be used in estimating take-up, and the take-up analyst has to make corresponding projections (see DSS, 1994b).

Administrative links between benefits

Chapter Two described overlaps and interactions at the structural level which might act towards depressing take-up by eligible people in some cases. This section pursues this further and considers how take-up may be affected by administrative links between different benefits and delivery systems. There are possibilities here for encouraging take-up.

The most obvious example is when receipt of one benefit serves as an automatic confirmation of entitlement to another. This might be expected to act towards increasing take-up of the second benefit, since it eliminates almost entirely the procedural hurdles. Results from the first survey of family income supplement claimants, shortly after introduction of this benefit, showed higher levels of take-up reported for all the benefits then 'passported' – (dental/optical and prescription charge exemptions, fares to hospital, welfare milk and school meals) – than among the same people before claiming family income supplement (Knight and Nixon, 1975).

At the client level, the effect of the administrative link is apparent in so far as the knowledge that passport benefits are available encourages take-up of the primary benefit entitlement, which appears more valuable. Several studies have shown that the availability of the passported health benefits can be the main reason for claiming family credit, especially relatively low entitlements (Corden and Craig, 1991; Noble *et al.*, 1992). However, the availability of passported health benefits can lead to complicated 'better-off' calculations which may also affect take-up decisions. For example, disabled working parents who might be able to choose between claiming family credit and disability working allowance, might take into account that health benefits were not passported by the latter benefit (House of Commons, 1993).

The extent to which benefits can be passported, or details from one application be transferred into another benefit administrative system, depends, of course, on the structure of the benefits, the extent to which eligibility criteria overlap, and the availability of a suitable mechanism for transfer. The multi-purpose claim form trials in the late 1970s offered applicants for one benefit the opportunity to claim a number of others at the same time (up to 14 in the Northern Ireland experiment, including supplementary benefit and family income supplement) (Peel, 1978; Graham and Brasier, 1979; Graham, 1980). The copying and distribution of the form was handled manually. The results of the experiments showed a limited effect on increasing take-up, at the expense of much greater administrative difficulty.

The advent of computerisation offered new opportunities in linking claimants' applications. Of particular importance is the link between the DSS administrative system and the local government administration of housing benefit, and council tax (community charge) benefits. Claims for income support are automatically notified to housing departments. While this eliminates some of the application procedure that could otherwise be necessary, the extent to which take-up is increased depends to some extent on the efficiency of the 'link' mechanism. A survey of local authorities in 1982 found that 72 per cent of respondents reported problems in matching housing benefit claim forms forwarded by the Benefits Agency with later information about whether income support had been awarded (Audit Commission, 1993). As explained before, new opportunities for increasing take-up always create new possibilities for confusion.

Whether or not administrative links do exist between benefits, claimants often expect that they will be told, automatically, of other entitlements, once they are in the system. This tends to inhibit enquiry (Ritchie and Matthews, 1982). Similarly, there may be an expectation that a change in circumstances notified to one benefit administration will be passed on to others (see Sainsbury *et al.*, 1995 forthcoming). Such an expectation was a reason for overpayment of housing benefit and community charge benefit (Audit Commission, 1993). How far the one-stop service approach can overcome some of these negative effects on take-up will depend on how good the administrative links can be made. One area where there is room for improvement is the underpayment of the severe disability premium in income support. Local studies have shown that non-take-up may be associated with poor procedural links between attendance allowance and income support administrators (Hayball, 1993; Alcock and Reid, 1994).

Computerised benefit records would seem to offer good opportunities for promotion of other benefits, but what seems simple has proved administratively hard in some cases. A postal survey of recipients of four disability benefits showed that a significant proportion would have liked to know about other schemes that might have been available to them (NAO, 1992). At the time of the study, 1990/91, the main computerised record of beneficiaries was unreliable for this purpose, however. Up to 20 per cent of people recorded as receiving attendance allowance had died. Hedges and Thomas (1994) showed how people with disabilities also wished that results from one medical examination could be passed on for other disability benefits.

Of particular interest is the possibility of using local authority administered benefit records for targeting other potential claimant populations, and promoting other benefits. Noble et al. (1992) urge a greater use of housing benefit records for targeted family credit take-up campaigns at a local level, an opportunity recognised earlier by Harlow District Council, who increased take-up of supplementary benefit and family income supplement by writing to families on the basis of information held on application forms for rent/rate rebates (Bennett, 1981).

The overlap between eligibility for housing benefit and family credit has received considerable attention. The tenure difference in take-up of family credit, with local authority tenants showing higher take-up, has been noted in several claimant studies (Noble *et al.*, 1992; Marsh and McKay, 1993). Dorsett and Heady (1991) used econometric techniques to look at the take-up of family income supplement and housing benefit over the period 1984–87, and modelled the interaction between the two. Those with large housing benefit entitlements were more likely to claim family income supplement as well as housing benefit. Dorsett and Heady made several suggestions as to why this might be happening: perhaps housing benefit was easier to claim than family income supplement, or families discovered family income supplement while claiming housing benefit, or perhaps housing benefit entitlement was a 'better indicator of poverty', because it included an element of housing costs?

Corden and colleagues have discussed another mechanism whereby applications for housing benefit may be driving applications for family credit (Corden *et al.*, 1993). The housing benefit guidance manual offers guidelines for dealing with 'notional family credit' for housing benefit applicants who have applied for but not received family credit, or are estimated by housing benefit officers to be eligible non-recipients of family credit who have not applied. It is not known how rigorously housing benefit officers follow this guidance. In the two local authority areas in which Noble *et al.* conducted their work on family credit take-up, they concluded that this issue was not very important. However, in a workshop with housing benefit officers from three authorities in the north of the country (Corden *et al.*, 1993) housing benefit officers explained that they systematically included notional family credit as income for assessment. They encouraged take-up of family credit where appropriate, when putting this rule into operation. For families with high entitlements of family credit, rigorous treatment of notional family credit in housing benefit assessment is a strong financial incentive to claim family credit. We might say that administration of housing benefit in these areas has an in-built component that would tend to encourage take-up of family credit.

Accuracy in decision making

The accuracy of decision making by adjudication officers will clearly affect the numbers of claimants and the amount of benefit claimed. Awards made to ineligible people will tend to inflate measures of take-up; if applications from eligible people are refused, take-up will be depressed. These direct administrative effects on the current potential population may also have subsequent effects at the client level on claimants' future decision making, for the same or other benefits.

The DSS conducts its own management checks on the level of error in decision making, and, of course, strives to reduce this wherever possible. Separate estimates of error in adjudication are made by the Chief Adjudication Officer, and by the National Audit Office, both for the Appropriation Accounts, and in separate enquiries on the administration of individual benefits. Rates of error are reported in different ways, and it is difficult to get a clear picture of the accuracy of decision making across a range of benefits. As an example of reported levels of error in some benefit adjudications, National Audit Office test examinations of income support payments during 1990–91 disclosed that some 13.6 per cent of cases scrutinised contained errors. Statistical extrapolations suggested that there had been overstatements of income support of £261.5 million, and understatements of £83.4 million (NAO, 1991c), which might be considered measures of overclaiming and non-take-up respectively.

The error rate in decisions that do not lead to awards are not scrutinised with as much care, however. Beltram observed that 'payments from public funds are traditionally documented, supervised and audited; decisions not to pay are not examined with equal care unless there is an appeal, or a complaint by an MP or other representative' (Beltram, 1984, p. 54). There is therefore no good evidence about the extent of non-take-up due to wrong decisions of ineligibility.

A particular area of concern has been the quality of medical decisions made in respect of applications for attendance and mobility allowances. During 1990–91, DSS decisions were overturned in 30 per cent of cases that went to Medical Boards, and 35 per cent of cases that were dealt with by Medical Appeal Tribunals (NAO, 1992). In two-thirds of the cases of rejections of attendance allowance that went for review, the original decisions were overturned in the applicant's favour. The DSS has always suggested that findings such as these are related to the extent to which medical conditions can change between separate assessments. However, the NAO monitoring board concluded that in nine per cent of cases monitored the Department's doctors had made major errors; that there was significant variation between different administrative centres and that part-time doctors showed highest rates of error. Take-up of attendance allowance and mobility allowance have undoubtedly been affected.

The effect of administrative error is currently attracting attention as a result of its significance within theory that underpins the statistical measurement of take-up (for example, Duclos, 1992). We return to this in the next section of the paper.

'Policing' the system

Finally, consideration of administrative effects on take-up returns to van Oorschot's schema. He identified one factor that enhanced the probability of occurrence of non-take-up as being the combination of service and fraud control functions in the same administrative scheme.

The fraudulent claiming of benefit by ineligible people is an aspect of take-up that is taken very seriously by the DSS. Cook (1991) describes the development of fraud control measures during the 1980s, suggesting that the primary aim was benefit savings. According to Cook, DSS investigative methods are geared to deterrence through stigmatisation and punishment of offenders (compared, for example, with tax evasion investigative measures geared more towards compliance). Exploring the discourse of benefit fraud, and the imagery created, helps to explain the popular concept of the benefit scrounger.

Research interviews with benefits staff and observations in local offices have demonstrated the extent to which abuse awareness had been inculcated in those who administered the system (Beltram, 1984; Cooper, 1985; Howe, 1985) and the effect that this had on decision making, particularly when discretionary decisions had to be made. Beltram (1984) described how local office managers and staff reacted to political emphasis on scrounging and well-publicised increases in the resources devoted to fraud control by getting tough, and this led to some restrictions on supplementary benefit payments. Howe (1985) went further in the emphasis he gave to the importance of fraud awareness. As a result of observing 75 staff/claimant interviews in a Northern Ireland social security office, he felt that the level of awareness of abuse was so high that local administrative practice gave practical priority to the prevention and detection of abuse, rather than being 'unambiguously devoted to the promotion of claimants' welfare' (p. 65). One simple example was rationing the supply of information literature. Howe thought it an inescapable conclusion that many claimants did not, and could not, get what they were theoretically entitled to, as a result of staff's commitment to prevention of abuse.

Fraud control affects take-up in a number of ways. Ineligible claimants are prevented or deterred, but eligible claimants as well are diverted or rejected after application. Potential claimants may never get as far as making an application for fear of scrutiny for possible abuse. Beltram pointed to pensioners as a group in which anxiety about the idea that they might be investigated, or, in such a complex scheme, make an inadvertent mistake, prevented applications. Other studies confirm the deterrent power of the imagery that has been cultivated in the prevention of fraud (Corden, 1983, 1987b; Corden and Craig, 1991; Boden and Corden, 1994) – an imagery that continues to be enthusiastically perpetuated (Craig, 1993).

There is little proper evidence about the extent of conscious fraudulent claiming, but we do know something about the circumstances under which benefit manipulation and fraudulent applications take place. Howe's analysis of interviews with unemployed claimants in Belfast (1993) showed how complex combinations of factors, including local labour market opportunities and traditional attitudes in local communities, acted together to remove the effective deterrence of being associated with working and claiming. Interviews conducted by Dean and Taylor Gooby (1991) and Jordan *et al.* (1992) offer further insights into the ways in which people construct their identities within current family and economic circumstances that effectively remove the personal stigmatisation of receiving benefit to which they are not officially entitled.

Another interesting example comes from the first year's experience of administering disability living allowance. It appears that large numbers of people claimed under the special rules arrangements (designed for people with terminal illness) in an attempt to short-circuit anticipated delays of intolerable length (House of Commons, 1993). An apparently resourceful attempt to obtain entitlement could properly be described as abusing the rules, and may well have prevented take-up by others truly entitled to the special rules arrangement, by competing for the overstretched resources. What is interesting is that administrative staff, sympathetic to the delays experienced, were also expediting particular applications under special rules procedures that were technically inappropriate.

These examples illustrate an interesting range of behaviour among both claimants and administrative staff in response to the administrative fraud control function of service. We know relatively little about claimants' conceptions of fraud, or manipulation of benefit rules. People behave in ways that seem rational to them; under certain circumstances they risk sanctions to protect their own interests; under other circumstances the deterrent effect of possible sanctions apparently dissolves. If take-up is to be properly understood from the supply side, there is a need for new research into the Department's current concept of fraud and fraud control functions, alongside research into the understanding and perceptions of the claimant population. The interaction of fraud control and service provision could be usefully re-examined, from the perspective of all the actors in the scene.

This brings to a conclusion the review of evidence of effects on take-up at the level of administration, organisation and delivery of benefits. Apart from a stream of interest in caseload patterns associated with advertising, there has been little effort so far to quantify these effects, although there are plenty of indications of their importance. However small the effect of one aspect of administration taken on its own, the cumulative effects at the client level may be considerable. What has also become clear is that every additional administrative procedure or promotional initiative may create opportunities to encourage take-up, but at the same time creates new possibilities of deterrence. One area of take-up that has begun to receive systematic quantitative attention is the effect of error in take-up estimates (Duclos, 1992; DSS, 1994b). We can expect this new focus of attention to stimulate new interest in the extent of, reasons for and effect of adjudication error.

'Intervening' in the administrative process

The final stream of work that must be considered in this review of take-up literature is that concerned with the role of take-up campaigns and welfare rights activities. We might call this intervention in the administrative procedure, either by promotion and information giving, direct advice and help to claimants, or advocacy and representation in the adjudication and appeal process. Take-up campaigns run by local authorities have been critically and comprehensively reviewed by Alcock and Shepherd (1987), and there is no point in replicating that work here. Earlier summaries of local activities were presented by Hill and Maunders (1985) and Falkingham (1986).

Alcock and Shepherd describe how the so-called blanket postcard campaigns initiated by Strathclyde Regional Council (Oliver and Melling, 1980) and quickly followed in Cleveland (1982) and Sandwell (1985) were designed as a deliberate mechanism to move the responsibility for taking up benefits by the client to responsibility for ensuring delivery of entitlement by the DHSS. From a welfare rights perspective the attraction of such campaigns lay in the possibility of 'reversing the pathological model of claimant inadequacy... and placing the problem of inadequate benefit delivery back with the state itself' (Alcock and Shepherd, 1987, p. 58), which has resonant echoes in van Oorschot's arguments for an approach to understanding take-up that lays more emphasis on supply side variables. And as Alcock and Shepherd trace the success of these campaigns in terms of the increased entitlements awarded, they remind us that all initiatives that increase take-up also have negative impacts, by describing the subsequent delays and confusion caused by the surges in applications stimulated by the blanket campaigns. These led to different approaches in subsequent campaigns – mediating the applications through welfare rights agencies, or targeting the campaigns more closely on specific groups such as elderly people (Harlow District Council, 1982) and ethnic minority groups (Khera, 1984; Leicester City Council, 1986).

The advantages of both blanket and targeted approaches were combined in a welfare rights research project commissioned by the DHSS in 1982. Personal approaches to randomly selected supplementary benefit claimants, with detailed benefits advice and assistance from an independent rights worker secured an increase in benefit in three-quarters of the cases investigated (Berthoud, 1984). How far benefits delivery should depend on the availability of independent advice and intervention remains controversial, however. Alcock and Shepherd argue that take-up campaigns, in fact, have acted to continue the isolation and alienation of claimants and reinforce pathological models of inadequacy, as well as disguising inadequacies within DSS delivery system. The role of welfare rights work within local authorities, and the apparent overlap with DSS responsibility has proved hard to evaluate (Berthoud *et al.*, 1986).

This concludes discussion about procedural aspects of the application and adjudication process that may influence take-up; and brings to an end the review of effects on take-up at the administrative level. The final chapter points to some conclusions that may be drawn from this review, and implications for benefit design and social security administration. The broader perspective on take-up that is achieved by setting supply-side issues alongside client-level aspects serves as a plank for discussion about the take-up concept itself. The author offers some preliminary observations at this stage, and raises some questions which she feels now need answering.

Conclusions and discussion: what next?

This paper has gone back to the research and literature on take-up, with the specific aim of emphasising 'supply-side' factors, to complement and bring up to date an earlier review by Craig (1991). The objective has been, wherever possible, to consider a wider perspective on take-up than the traditional approach in research, which has concentrated rather narrowly on non-take-up by people with entitlements. Thus we have included important findings about ineligible people who make unsuccessful applications as well as people who claim benefits while technically ineligible. The distinctions between eligible and ineligible people, claimants and non-claimants are technicalities for social security provision but are often artificial distinctions in the wider context of people's lives and their social and economic environment. The low-income population is fluid; individual and family circumstances are constantly changing in a variety of ways; benefit rules and administrative procedures are subject to constant revision. A narrow focus on non-take-up by eligible people is likely to limit understanding and obscure aspects of importance.

The framework for this review has been influenced by models and schemas that offer alternatives to previous individualistic models of the decision making process, especially van Oorschot's suggestion that there are three all important levels of influence on take-up. Client behaviour – how individuals respond to the available provision – is the most apparent direct influence on take-up. This has been the traditional focus of research interest, albeit with emphasis on people with entitlement to the provision. Craig's review of research and literature on take-up was grounded within the client level approach, and we have not sought to replicate his comprehensive work.

The focus in this review has been on the other two levels of influence which, van Oorschot argues, it is as important to include in attempts to understand take-up. Going back to the research and literature on take-up to see what is known about the effects of benefit structure and administrative features, called here 'supply-side factors', both broadens our understanding and shows some important gaps in current knowledge.

There appears to be evidence to support van Oorschot's thesis that structural aspects of benefit design have indirect effects on take-up by setting the parameters for administration and client response, and that these must be considered. Similarly, the review has shown that there can be direct administrative effect on take-up (for example, wrong decisions) as well as a whole range of administrative aspects which act indirectly by influencing people's claiming behaviour.

All three levels of influence are important, and all are interlinked. A means-test, for example, is a structural feature devised at policy level. As such, it both determines the parameters for administrative implementation, and helps to shape the range of possible responses and decision making by people who might claim. The way in which the means-test is put into operation by the administrators is also influential. At the client level, people's experience of a means-test depends on individual attitudes, beliefs and feelings derived from a range of experiences spanning whole lives.

Understanding the different levels of influence requires appropriate conceptualisation and different modes of enquiry at each of the three levels, as well as clarification of the ways in which factors at different levels are linked. The rest of this chapter looks at some of the policy implications of these conclusions for benefit design and administrative process, and ends by suggesting a new look at the current conceptualisation of take-up.

Benefit design

In so far as individual benefit structures incorporate aspects that, indirectly, tend to depress take-up, it may be hard to approach the required balance – maximum possible levels of receipt by entitled people and minimum achievable levels of applications and receipt by people without entitlement. This is especially important in view of the increasing commitment to targeting. Van Oorschot's work suggests, and the research evidence generally supports this view, that those structural features which are required in order to reach particular low-income groups or particular sets of personal circumstances, are likely to be just those features which may be associated with depressed take-up by eligible people, or inflated applications from ineligible people.

In certain benefit schemes, structure and design are such that maintaining take-up levels is likely to require continuous, vigorous, promotional effort and high levels of administrative resourcing, and it is likely to be difficult to reduce adjudication error. The balance point, between the take-up and error rates on one side, and the administrative resourcing on the other, will depend on current policy emphasis. It will be situated differently for each benefit, according to demographic and economic changes and political requirements. The balance point will also depend on the extent to which responsibility for promotion and operationalisation is shared beyond the policy makers/administrator/client nexus. At the moment a range of third parties are drawn in.

There are good reasons for such diversity of responsibility and involvement. It means, however, that some of the direct financial costs are borne outside the DSS, and beyond the claimant. As we go deeper into the market economy we can expect this to attract greater attention. How long can we expect a supply of 'free' information to the DSS, for example, from employers confirming earnings levels, or social workers supporting social fund applications? How long will the supply of free information and advice to claimants continue at the current level? Changes in these supplies and costs of information and advice would certainly affect take-up and, indeed, would have major implications for operationalising social security. It is not too early to start to think about such issues. The momentum towards implementing community care strategies has re-opened some debate about the sharing of responsibility for maintaining take-up (for example, Greeves, 1994; Griffiths, 1994) and it would be useful to insert into this debate aspects of benefit design and structure.

Administration

The review has made it clear that every aspect of administration can potentially affect take-up. Each new initiative to increase administrative efficiency, including those initiatives specifically designed to increase take-up, also has the potential to act towards depressing take-up in some cases. For example, every advertisement to encourage take-up by eligible people also carries the risk of being interpreted in a way that puts some eligible people off and suggests to some ineligible people that they should apply. If resources directed towards new technologies for provision of information and advice can only be made available if withdrawn from other areas of promotional activity, then we can expect effects which increase take-up among some groups and depress it among others.

The 'one stop service' approach proposed by the Benefits Agency as a recent initiative to increase effectiveness and customer service is also likely to have both positive and negative effects on take-up. If this can provide a whole person approach, and levels of resourcing can maintain highly trained staff, complex computer interaction and easily accessible telephone links, then this will act towards increasing take-up in some cases. To the extent that the approach depends on people taking initiatives themselves to get in touch, then the one stop service may have little immediate effect on take-up by the housebound, or those without a telephone. The location and number of the 'shops' may be critical. Since we know that telephone switchboards and computer links will be dysfunctional occasionally, and staff required to provide comprehensive, complex information will occasionally be inadequate for the task, then there may be effects that act towards depressing take-up. In so far as the expensive new initiative draws resources away from home visiting (or any other current activity found helpful) then, eventually, there will be deterrent effects on some groups of people. A client group approach may have positive effects for those people who identify positively with the labels offered, for example, some pensioners. It is likely to have negative effects for those whose circumstances overlap the administrative groups, or who do not like being identified in such ways (Adler and Sainsbury, 1993). The higher the expectations raised by the one stop provision then the greater the frustration and disappointment when these are not met.

The concept of take-up

The general theme of this review has been that a broader conceptualisation of take-up is now needed. The author perceives two possible stumbling blocks here, and offers these for discussion. The first is that, linguistically, 'take-up' and hence 'take-up measure' or 'take-up estimate' is terminology rooted at the client level. The second aspect is the possibly inflated status and usefulness of the 'take-up measure' as a major indicator of outcome of the whole process, for some benefits.

First, the term 'take-up' itself (and hence, measure or estimate of take-up) is derived from activity at the client level. It is the claimant who 'takes up' the benefit. The review has shown however, that 'take-up' is also the direct result of administrative decision making, and that indirect effects of benefit structure and administration are also powerful influences. Only one of these three levels of influence is captured linguistically by the terminology in use. This might indeed be another contributory factor leading to the concentration of research interest in client-level models, discussed in the first chapter. The linguistic derivation of the word itself may have constrained our conceptualisation. There is room for speculation as to whether research and thinking about take-up would have gone down different avenues if the word used to describe what we call 'take-up' had been, instead, 'inclusion' – a word which would encompass decision making and activity at all three levels of influence, and would accommodate discretionary schemes. It seems likely that a terminology of 'exclusion', rather than non-take-up, would have led to different kinds of research, and indeed, different conceptualisations.

This is not an argument for just substituting now a different term for 'take-up'. Attempts to shift conceptualisation of social security by purposeful linguistic changes may be less than helpful in increasing our understanding of the processes at work. For example, those who have been continuously engaged on research on claiming behaviour in low-income families since the 1970s have observed the shifts in policy makers' preferred language from 'applicant' to 'claimant' to 'customer'. Transcripts from research interviews and group discussions spanning this period show clearly that the experience, for many of those so described, remains one of 'putting in for it', 'giving it a try', 'having a go', or 'asking the social'. There is a wide gap between conceptualisation of the process as expressed in this kind of language and conceptualisation of the process of being 'a customer'. Understanding take-up requires acknowledgement and investigation of these different streams of discourse, rather than suggestions for new forms of words. So the argument is not for a new word for 'take-up', but for greater understanding of the possible influence of the term through its linguistic derivation.

Moving on from the suggestion that our conceptualisation of take-up may have been constrained by the terminology of the discourse, it may also be useful to reconsider the status of the take-up measure (or take-up estimate), and to consider whether we need to be more critical of this if we are to make progress in understanding the process of take-up itself. The present review was not primarily concerned with measures of take-up, as such, because Craig (1991) gave this topic comprehensive coverage. It is appropriate to reintroduce the topic here, however, in this final discussion. The introduction to the review explained why measures of take-up were considered so important in policy evaluation. The traditional use of the take-up estimate has been as an indicator of current policy effectiveness. It has been used to show how some people do (and do not) respond to social security provisions designed to increase incomes, raise living standards and influence behaviour. It serves as a 'performance indicator' of current policy in a variety of ways, and a take-up measure that can be used predictively is considered a useful tool if it can also be predicted fairly accurately.

The value of the take-up measure or estimate (as with any measure) depends on its accuracy. The review has drawn attention to recent work that is starting to reveal the possible inaccuracy of the measures as currently estimated, and we have included in this discussion the level of erroneous decision making by adjudication officers. The Government's own statisticians have recently stated that, for income-related benefits, recent developments in understanding of the issues involved confirm that 'there is a potential for take-up estimates to be highly inaccurate' (Harris, 1994 p. 1). Recognition of possible inaccuracies has already led the DSS to adopt a new way of presenting estimates of take-up, using ranges rather than point estimates (DSS, 1994b) and suggesting that only broad assumptions about trends in take-up over time are possible.

While such 'ranges' and 'broad assumptions' may be more realistic indicators, it seems possible that their relative lack of precision may reduce their usefulness and traditional status. What will happen to the concept of take-up now that the possibility of accurate measurement of a take-up rate seems to be fading?

Leaving aside, however, the question of accuracy, we can also ask whether the measure is conceptually as useful as the attention it has received would suggest. The measure seems unsophisticated. First, there is no parameter of time. The length of time spent as an eligible non-claimant may be a more important indicator of either poverty or policy effectiveness than current claiming status for some benefits. Marsh and McKay made the interesting observation that the current take-up measure for family credit actually excluded those families for whom the benefit may have been most effective, in that families moving rapidly through eligibility to higher net incomes within a six month award period were not counted (1993, p. 75). In the traditional, caseload-based take-up measure a family not claiming £50 per week for six months 'scores' the same as a family who has failed to claim £5 for two weeks.

The expenditure-based measure of take-up takes account of the value of entitlement, but again has no time parameters, and has its own limitations. If a benefit overlaps with another, expenditure-based take-up indicates only expenditure by the DSS and not financial value to recipients. Noble *et al.* (1992) suggested that a 'net worth' figure taking into account reductions in housing benefit and community charge benefit could be more useful in assessing take-up of family credit, or the extent to which families were missing out if not claiming.

None of these measures, however, is appropriate for benefits where discretionary administrative decisions determine eligibility of individual people, primarily the important social fund. Lack of a traditional take-up measure as a basis for research and discussion may have constrained, to some extent, evaluation and debate of the social fund. There may well be similar constraints developing in our conceptualisation of take-up of new disability benefits where eligibility criteria include self-assessment of disability.

While current versions of take-up measures begin to seem crude and inadequate, this is not an argument for directing resources increasingly towards refining traditional measures or searching for new techniques to improve their accuracy. By elevating the status of the current take-up measure, this could obscure the need for other appropriate indicators of outcome. Included here is the need for an outcome measure for participation of ineligible people. The review has emphasised the importance of ineligible applicants in a broader conceptualisation of take-up. For some benefits, such people outnumber those who are represented within the current take-up measure.

Current take-up measures tell us only about receipt of benefit, not outcomes in terms of effectiveness in maintaining real living standards or otherwise. Yet it is currently easy to assume, from the attention paid to 'improving take-up' that increased take-up means increased welfare. Marsh and McKay's recent findings (1993) that a group of family credit claimants scored higher on an index of relative material hardship than a group of eligible non-claimants, underline the need for additional different kinds of outcome measures.

It seems that the current crude and increasingly inadequate 'take-up measure' might assume a different but appropriate place and status among a range of other informative and useful outcome measures, if we moved towards a broader conceptualisation of take-up.

This final section of the review has raised more questions than it has provided answers. The hope is that this may help to stimulate further discussion. Despite all the attention paid to 'take-up' in the past thirty years, the author believes that there is scope for a major move forwards, away from the traditional concept of take-up towards one that is more broadly based. We would then be better equipped to decide which of the components to monitor, and the best way to assess or measure each of these. Appropriate outcome measures other than the traditional 'take-up estimate' might well emerge from this, which would be more useful to policy analysis, and reflect more accurately current levels of knowledge.

References

ADLER, M. and DU FEU, D. (1975) A computer based welfare benefit information system – the Inverclyde project, IBM.

ADLER, M. and SAINSBURY, R. (1993) 'The 'one-stop shop': haven't we been here before?' *Benefits*, 6, Jan/Feb, 35–37.

AGE CONCERN (1992a) *Age Concern England's Comments to the Social Security Committee Enquiry into Disability Benefit*, London: Age Concern England.

AGE CONCERN (1992b) *Age Concern Questionnaire on Benefits Administration*, London: Age Concern England.

ALCOCK, P. and REID, P. (1994) 'Taking charge', *Community Care*, 1014, 28.

ALCOCK, P. and SHEPHERD, J. (1987) 'Take-up campaigns: fighting poverty through the post', *Critical Social Policy*, 19, 52–67.

ALCORN, D. and SMITH, M. (1985) *Computerised Welfare Rights*, report of a twelve month project, Belfast: Community Information Service.

AMIN, K. with OPPENHEIM, C. (1992) *Poverty in Black and White: Deprivation and Ethnic Minorities*, London: Child Poverty Action Group and Runnymede Trust.

ASHWORTH, K. and WALKER, R. (1992) *Family Credit: Aspects of a Changing Caseload*, Centre for Research in Social Policy, Loughborough University of Technology.

ATKINSON, A.B. with CHAMPION, B. (1989) 'Family income supplement and two parent families 1971–80' in Atkinson, A.B. *Poverty and Social Security*, Hemel Hempstead: Harvester Wheatsheaf.

AUDIT COMMISSION (1993) *Remote Control: the national administration of housing benefit*, London: HMSO.

AUSTIN, N., SMITH, N. and BRYSON, C. (1994) *The Benefits Agency National Customer Survey, 1993*, Leeds: Public Attitude Surveys Ltd/Benefits Agency.

BA (1992) *One Stop Shop: Benefits Agency service delivery – a discussion paper*, Benefits Agency, Leeds.

BA (1994) Benefits Agency – *Who we are and what we do*, Benefits Agency, Leeds.

BARNARDOS (1990) *Missing the Target*, Essex: Barnardos.

BATEMAN, N, (1992) 'Computers – Empowering the user', *Benefits*, 5, 37.

BECKER, S. and SILBURN, R. (1990) *The New Poor Clients. Social Work, Poverty and the Social Fund*, Wellington: Community Care and Benefit Research Unit.

BELTRAM, G. (1984) *Testing the Safety Net: An Enquiry into the Reformed Supplementary Benefit Scheme*, London: Bedford Square Press/NCVO.

BENNETT, T. (1981) *Making People Better Off*, Community Services Department, Harlow District Council, Essex.

BERESFORD, B. (1994) *Positively Parents: Caring for a Severely Disabled Child*, SPRU Papers, London: HMSO.

BERTHOUD, R. (1984) *The Reform of Supplementary Benefit, Working Papers*, London: Policy Studies Institute.

BERTHOUD, R., BENSON, S. and WILLIAMS, S. (1986) *Standing up for Claimants. Welfare rights work in local authorities*, London: Policy Studies Institute.

BLOCH, A. (1992) *Access to Service and Benefit Information: Needs of Ethnic Minority Groups*, London: Policy Studies Institute.

BLUNDELL, R.W., FRY, U.C. and WALKER, I. (1988) Modelling the take-up of means-tested benefits in the UK: the case of housing benefits, *Economic Journal*, 98, 58–94.

BODEN, R. and CORDEN, A. (1994) *Measuring Low Incomes: Self-employment and Family Credit*, SPRU Papers, London: HMSO.

BOLITHO (1976) *Family Income Supplement. The Effect of Publicity on Take-up of Benefit*, DHSS internal paper, mimeograph.

BRIGGS, E. and REES, A.M. (1980) *Supplementary Benefits and the Consumer*, Occasional Papers on Social Administration No. 65, London: Bedford Square Press.

BUCKLAND, S. and DAWSON, P. (1989) 'Household claiming behaviour', *Social Policy and Administration*, 23, 60–71.

BUCKLE, J. (1988) *Am I Entitled?* London: Disablement Income Group.

CASSERLEY, J. and CLARK, B. (1977) *A Welfare Rights Approach to the Chronically Sick and Disabled*, Strathclyde Social Work Department.

CLEVELAND COUNTY COUNCIL (1982) *The Welfare Benefits Campaign*, Middlesborough: Cleveland County Social Services Division.

COHEN, R. (1983) *Able to claim?*, London: Islington People's Rights.

COHEN, R. and TARPEY, M. (1982) *The Trouble with Take-up*, London: Islington People's Rights.

COHEN, R., COXALL, J., CRAIG, G. and SADIQ-SANGSTER, A. (1992) *Hardship Britain: Being Poor in the 1990s*, London: Child Poverty Action Group.

COI (1989) *Family Credit: Spring 1989 Campaign Evaluation Management Summary*, Central Office of Information Research Unit, (mimeo).

COI (1990) *Family Credit: Adjusting Strategy Development*, verbal presentation to Central Office of Information, 2 March, Andrew Irving Associates, (mimeo).

COOK, D. (1991) 'Social injustice: the differential enforcement of tax and social security regulations', in Adler, M., Bell, C., Clasen, J. and Sinfield, A. (eds) *The Sociology of Social Security*, Edinburgh: Edinburgh University Press.

COOPER, S. (1985) Working paper C (Work in local offices). *The Reform of Supplementary Benefit*, London: Policy Studies Institute.

CORDEN, A. (1983) *Taking up a Means Tested Benefit. The Process of Claiming Family Income Supplement*, London: HMSO.

CORDEN, A. (1987a) *Disappointed Applicants. A Study of Unsuccessful Claims for Family Income Supplement*, Aldershot: Avebury.

CORDEN, A. (1987b) 'Claiming behaviour and take-up: a model for people with mental handicap', *British Journal of Mental Subnormality*, 33, 64: 57–65.

CORDEN, A. (1991) 'Women's business?', *Poverty*, 80, 1, 9–11.

CORDEN, A. (1992) 'A qualitative study of self-employed recipients of family credit', DSS 963, Social Policy Research Unit Working Paper, University of York.

CORDEN, A. and CRAIG, P. (1991) *Perceptions of Family Credit*, SPRU Papers, London: HMSO.

CORDEN, A., EARDLEY, T., SMELLIE, R. with ELLIOTT, J. (1993) *Housing benefit for self-employed people: report of a group discussion with local authority officers*, DSS 1048, Social Policy Research Unit Working Paper, University of York.

COSTIGAN, P., RITCHIE, J. and WHITE, C. (1992) *Allowances and Pensions for Disability*, London: Social and Community Planning Research, for National Audit Office.

COWELL, F.A. (1986) *Welfare Benefits and the Economics of Take-up*, ESRC Programme on taxation, incentives and the distribution of income, Discussion Paper 89, London School of Economics.

CRAIG, G. (1990) 'Watching the social fund', in Manning, N. and Ungerson, C. (eds) *Social Policy Review 1989–90*, Harlow: Longman.

CRAIG, G. (1992) *Replacing the Social Fund, A Strategy for Change*, York: Social Policy Research Unit.

CRAIG, G. (1993) 'Behold the Lord High Executioner', *Benefits*, 6, 57–58.

CRAIG, P. (1991) 'Costs and benefits: a review of research on take-up of income-related benefits', *Journal of Social Policy*, 20, 4: 537–566.

DAVIES, B. and REDDIN, M. (1978) *Universality, Selectivity and Effectiveness in Social Policy*, London: Heinemann.

DAVIES, C. and RITCHIE, J. (1988) *Tipping the Balance. A Study of Non take-up of Benefits in an Inner City Area*, London: HMSO.

DAVIS, A. (1984) 'Welfare rights and mentally ill people', *Social Services Research*, December 1984, 77–86.

DAWSON, P., BUCKLAND, S. and GILBERT, N. (1990) 'Expert systems and the public provision of welfare benefit advice', *Policy and Politics*, 18, 1: 43–54.

DAY, G. (1985) 'Promoting take-up of benefits by the mentally handicapped', *Municipal Review and AMA News*, 55, 655: 222–223.

DEACON, A. and BRADSHAW, J. (1983) *Reserved for the Poor: The Means Test in British Social Policy*, Oxford: Blackwell and Robertson.

DEAN, H. and TAYLOR GOOBY, P. (1992) *Dependency Culture: The Explosion of a Myth*, Hemel Hempstead: Harvester Wheatsheaf.

DHSS (1984) *Service to the Public: Report on take up of benefit project at adult training centres*, London: Department of Health and Social Security.

DHSS (1985) *Reform of Social Security: Programme for Action*, Department of Social Security, White Paper, Cmnd 9691, London: HMSO.

DONOHEW, L., TIPTON, L. and HANEY, R. (1978) 'Analysis of information seeking strategies', *Journalism Quarterly*, 55, 15–31.

DORSETT, R. and HEADY, C. (1991) 'The take-up of means-tested benefits by working families with children', *Fiscal Studies*, 12, 4: 22–32.

DSS (1993a) *The growth of social security*, Department of Social Security, London: HMSO.

DSS (1993b) *Income related benefits: estimates of take-up in 1989*, Analytical Services Division, London: Government Statistical Service.

DSS (1994a) *The Government's expenditure plans 1994–95 to 1996–97*, Social Security Departmental Report, Cm 2513, London: HMSO.

DSS (1994b) *Income related benefits: estimates of take-up in 1990 and 1991*, Analytical Services Division, London: Government Statistical Service.

DUCLOS, J-Y. (1992) *The take-up of state benefits: an application to supplementary benefit in Britain using the FES*, WSP/71, Welfare State Programme, London: School of Economics.

EARDLEY, T. (1993) 'The living standards of self-employed family credit recipients: a qualitative study', DSS 1055, Social Policy Research Unit Working Paper, University of York.

EPSTEIN, J. (1984) *New Technology, New Entitlement*, London: Research Institute for Consumer Affairs.

FALKINGHAM, F. (1985) *Take-up of Benefit: A Literature Review*, University of Nottingham: Benefits Research Unit.

FRY, V. and STARK, G. (1993) *The take-up of means tested benefits, 1984–90*, London: Institute of Fiscal Studies.

GIGG, D. (1983) *Evaluation of Revised Postal Claim Form and National Introduction of School Leaver Postal Claim Form*, Central Management Services, DHSS.

GORDON, P. and NEWNHAM, A. (1985) *Passport to benefits? Racism in social security*, London: Child Poverty Action Group and The Runnymede Trust.

GRAHAM, J. (1980) *The Multi-Purpose Claim Form Trial in Northern Ireland*, Belfast: Policy Planning and Research Unit, Department of Finance.

GRAHAM, J. (1984) *Take-up of Family Income Supplement. Knowledge, Attitudes and Experience – Claimants and Non-claimants*, Occasional Paper 2, Belfast: Policy Planning and Research Unit.

GRAHAM, S. and BRASIER, F. (1979) *The Multi-Purpose Claim Form Trial in Brighton*, London: Social Research Branch, Department of Health and Social Security.

GREEVES, B. (1994) 'Welcoming the cavalry? The inter-relationship of local authorities with the Benefits Agency', *Benefits*, 10, 28–29.

GREGORY, P. (1993) 'The Citizen's Charter and the DSS', *Benefits*, 6, 29–30.

GRIFFITHS, S. (1994) 'Primary care – a setting for benefits take-up', *Benefits*, 10, 27–28.

HANSARD (1980) House of Commons, 27 November, col. 213, written answer.

HANSARD (1992) House of Commons, 14 May, cols. 181–2, written answer.

HARDIE, A. and MILLER, G. (1985) 'Reaping the benefits', *Health and Social Service Journal*, 24 January, 105–6.

HARLOW DISTRICT COUNCIL (1982) *Gaining Benefits from Day Care*, Research Report, Harlow District Council.

HARPER, K. (1993) 'Stiffer claims target 'to cut jobless total'', *The Guardian*, 26 May.

HARRIS, G. (1994) *The take-up of income related benefits: inaccuracies in the estimation of take-up rates*, Analytical Note 3, Analytical Services Division, Department of Social Security, London.

HARRIS, J. (forthcoming) 'Contract and citizenship in social welfare: 1934–48', *Journal of Political Ideology*.

HAYBALL, J. (1993) 'Promoting take-up amongst home care clients', *Benefits*, 8, Sept/Oct, 34–35.

HEDGES, A. (1988) *Social security literature – evaluation of social security written material*, Report on a preliminary qualitative study, Leighton Buzzard.

HEDGES, A. and THOMAS, A. with KEEGAN, J. and DULDIG, W. (1994) *Making a Claim for Disability Benefits*, Department of Social Security Research Report No. 27, London: HMSO.

HILL, B. and MAUNDERS, S. (1983) *Benefit take-up campaign*, Conference report, Leicester City Council.

HILL, M. (1976) 'Access to benefits in the welfare state', in *The State, Administration and the Individual*, London/Glasgow: Fontana/ Collins.

HINKLEY, P. (1992) *Health Information Services for Senior Citizens*, Information Policy Working Paper 4, London: Policy Studies Institute.

HOUSE OF COMMONS (1982) *Administrative Forms in Government*, Cmnd 8504, London: HMSO.

HOUSE OF COMMONS (1993) *Disability benefits: the delivery of disability living allowance and disability working allowance*, Third Report of the Social Security Committee, Session 1992–93.

HOWE, L.E.A. (1985) 'The deserving and the undeserving. Practice in an urban local social security office', *Journal of Social Policy*, 14, 1: 49–72.

HOWE, L. (1990) *Being Unemployed in Northern Ireland*, Cambridge: Cambridge University Press.

HUBY, M. and DIX, G. (1992) *Evaluating the Social Fund*, Department of Social Security Research Report No. 9, London: HMSO.

HUTSON, S. and JENKINS, R. (1989) *Taking the Strain: Family, Unemployment and the Transition to Adulthood*, Milton Keynes: Open University Press.

JARMAN, B. (1985) 'Giving advice about welfare benefits in general practice', *British Medical Journal*, 290: 522–524.

JORDAN, B., JONES, S., KAY, H. and REDLEY, M. (1992) *Trapped in Poverty: Labour market divisions in low income households*, London: Routledge.

KEMPSON, E. (1985) *Designing public documents: a review of research and other documents*, commissioned by the DHSS Information Division, unpublished.

KERR, S. (1982) 'Deciding about supplementary pensions: a provisional model', *Journal of Social Policy*, 11, 4: 505–17.

KERR, S. (1983) *Making Ends Meet: An Investigation into the Non-Claiming of Supplementary Pensions*, London: Bedford Square Press.

KHERA, R. (1984) *Report of the Sandwell Welfare Rights Take-up Campaign with Respect to Asian Minorities*, Sandwell Citizens Advice Bureau.

KNIGHT, J.B. and NIXON, J.M. (1975) *Two Parent Families in Receipt of Family Income Supplement 1972*, DHSS Statistical and Research Reports, No.9, London: HMSO.

LAW, I., HYLTON, C., KARMANI, A. and DEACON, A. (1993) *Racial equality and social security service delivery*, Working Paper 10, School of Sociology and Social Policy, University of Leeds.

LEEMING, A. and UNELL, J. (1992) *Benefit Information Needs of Lone Parents*, Discussion Paper 171, Centre for Research in Social Policy, Loughborough University of Technology.

LEICESTER CITY COUNCIL (1986) *The Braunstone Campaign*, Leicester City Council.

LYNES, T. (1991) 'Drumming up new business', *Community Care*, 11 July, 9.

MARSH, A. and MCKAY, S. (1993) *Families, Work and Benefits*, London: Policy Studies Institute.

MARTIN, J.M. and GIGG, D. (1983) *National introduction of postal claim form: evaluation and monitoring*, Central Management Services, DHSS.

MCLAUGHLIN, E. (1991) *Social Security and Community Care: The Case of the Invalid Care Allowance*, Department of Social Security Research Report No. 4, London: HMSO.

MCLAUGHLIN, E., MILLAR, J. and COOKE, K. (1989) *Work and Welfare Benefits*, Aldershot: Avebury.

MCLAUGHLIN, E., RITCHIE, J. and WALKER, R. (1990) *The Claiming of Social Security Benefits*, paper presented to IRISS Conference 1990, CP 673, Social Policy Research Unit, University of York.

MILLAR, J. and COOKE, K. (1984) *A Study of the Take-up of One Parent Benefit in Hackney*, DHSS 227, Social Policy Research Unit Working Paper, University of York.

MOFFITT, R. (1983) 'An economic model of welfare stigma', *American Economic Review*, 73: 1023–35.

MORI (1990) *Income Support: A Survey of Low Income Families*, research conducted for National Audit Office, London.

NACAB (1990a) *Hard Times For Social Fund Applicants*, London: National Association of Citizens Advice Bureaux.

NACAB (1990b) *Assessing the Assessors*, London: National Association of Citizens Advice Bureaux.

NACAB (1991) *Barriers to Benefit*, London: National Association of Citizens Advice Bureaux.

NAO (1985) *Department of Health and Social Security, Arrangements for Delivery of Social Security Benefits*, London: HMSO.

NAO (1991a) *The Social Fund*, London: HMSO.

NAO (1991b) *Support for Low Income Families*, London: HMSO.

NAO (1991c) *National Audit Office: Appropriation Accounts 1990–91,* Class XIV, Vote 2: Income Support, London: National Audit Office.

NAO (1992) *Quality of Service: War pensions, mobility allowance, attendance allowance and invalid care allowance*, London: HMSO.

NAO (1993) *Quality of Service: Income Support for Self-employed and Formerly Self-employed People*, London: HMSO.

NCC (1983) *Social Security: A Consumer Review*, working papers of the joint Consumer Councils' Social Security Committee, London: National Consumer Council.

NOBLE, M., SMITH, G. and MUNBY, T. (1992) *The Take-up of Family Credit*, Department of Applied Social Studies and Social Research, University of Oxford.

NOP (1990) *A Survey Among Family Credit Recipients*, London: NOP Market Research.

OLIVER, Q. and MELLING, G. (1980) 'Strathclyde pulls out all the stops', *Community Care*, 28 August.

OORSCHOT, W. VAN (1991) 'Non-take-up of social security benefits in Europe', *Journal of European Social Policy*, 1 (1), 15–30.

OORSCHOT, W. VAN (1995) *Realizing Rights*, Aldershot: Avebury.

OORSCHOT, W. VAN and SCHELL, J. (1991) 'Means testing in Europe: a growing concern', in Adler, M., Bell, C., Clasen, J. and Sinfield, A. (eds) *The Sociology of Social Security*, Edinburgh: Edinburgh University Press.

OORSCHOT, W. VAN and KOLKHUIS TANCKE, P. (1989) Niet-gebruik van sociale Zekerheid; feiten, theorieen, onderzoeksmethoden, CO52-series, no.16, Den Haag, Netherlands.

OTLEY, P. and KEMPSON, E. (1982) *Computer Benefits?*, London: National Consumer Council.

PEEL, J. (1978) *The Multi-Purpose Claim Form Trial in Salop*, Social Research Branch, Department of Health and Social Security, London.

PERKINS, E., ROBERTS, S. and MOORE, N. (1992) *Helping Clients Claim Their Benefits. The Information Needs of Informal Benefits Advisers*, London: Policy Studies Institute.

PERKINS, L. (1991) *Document Design for the Visually Handicapped*, London: Policy Studies Institute.

PHILLIPS, H. and GLENDINNING, C. (1981) *Who Benefits?*, London: The Disability Alliance.

PINKER, R. (1971) *Social Theory and Social Policy*, London: Heinemann.

POIRRIER, R. (1993) *Public information provided by social security institutions: current practice in social security and its users*, Studies in Research No.33, Geneva: International Social Security Association.

RITCHIE, J. and ENGLAND, J. (1985) *The Hackney Benefit Study: A Study to Investigate the Take-up of Means-Tested Benefits Within the London Borough of Hackney*, unpublished report, Social and Community Planning Research, London.

RITCHIE, J. and MATTHEWS, A. (1982) *Take-up of Rent Allowances: An In-depth Study*, London: Social and Community Planning Research.

ROGERS, E. with SHOEMAKER, F. (1971) *Communication of Innovations: a cross-cultural approach*, London: Collier Macmillan.

ROWLANDS, I. (1991) *Designing Public Documents: a review of research 1988–1990*, unpublished, London: Policy Studies Institute.

SAINSBURY, R., DITCH, J. and HUTTON, S. (1993) *Changing Circumstances of Income Support Recipients: Review of Selected Literature*, DSS 1076, Social Policy Research Unit Working Paper, University of York.

SAINSBURY, R., HUTTON, S. and DITCH, J. (1995 forthcoming) *Changing Circumstances and the Role of Income Support*, Department of Social Security Research Report Series, London: HMSO.

SANDWELL (1985) *Benefiting Sandwell: Campaign 1982–84*, West Midlands County Council.

SAUNDERS, P. (1990) *Selectivity and targeting in income support: the Australian experience*, Discussion Paper 17, Social Policy Research Centre, University of New South Wales, Australia.

SILKE, D. (1992) *Researching the Disability Working Allowance Self Assessment Form*, Department of Social Security Research Report No. 13, London: HMSO.

SMITH, R. (1990) *Under the Breadline*, London: Children's Society.

SOCIAL TRENDS (1994) Central Statistical Office, London: HMSO.

STEWART, G. and STEWART, J. (1991) *Relieving Poverty*, London: Association of Metropolitan Authorities.

STEWART, G., STEWART, J., PRIOR, A. and PEELO, M. (1989) *Surviving Poverty*, Wakefield: Association of Chief Officers of Probation.

STEWART, J. (ed) (1989) *Welfare Rights in Social Work Education*, London: CCCTSW.

STRAUSS, R.P. (1977) 'Information and participation in a public transfer programme', *Journal of Public Economics*, 8: 385–96.

SUMPTON, R. (1985) 'Welfare benefits for people with a mental handicap: the professional's role', *British Journal of Mental Subnormality*, 31, 60 (1): 3–7.

TARPEY, M. (1984) *English Speakers Only: A Report of Work on Take-up of Social Security Benefits with People Whose First Language was not English*, London: Islington People's Rights.

TAYLOR-GOOBY, P. (1994) 'Postmodernism and Social Policy: a great leap backwards?', *Journal of Social Policy*, 23, 3, 385–404.

TITMUSS, R. (1968) *Commitment to welfare*, London: Allen and Unwin.

TOOK, M. J. (1983a) 'Claiming supplementary benefit by post', *Management in Government*, 2: 120–124.

TOOK, M.J. (1983b) 'Forms improvement in DHSS', *Management in Government*, 1983, 3: 185-190.

VICTOR, C.R. (1985) *How Effective are Benefit Take-up Campaigns with the Elderly?* paper presented to British Society of Gerontology Conference, Keele, September.

VINCENT, J., ASHWORTH, K. and WALKER, R. (1991) *Taking Account of Time in the Targeting and Administration of Benefits*, Discussion Paper 141, Centre for Research in Social Policy, Loughborough University of Technology.

WALKER, R. (1980) *Thoughts Provoked by the Paper on Take-up*, note delivered to a Department of Environment Seminar, 13 April.

WALKER, R. (in association with Ashworth, K.) (1994) *Poverty Dynamics: Issues and Examples*, Aldershot: Avebury.

WALKER, R., DIX, G. and HUBY, M. (1992) *Working the Social Fund*, Department of Social Security Research Report No.8, London: HMSO.

WARDER, J. and ENGLAND, J. (1981) *Social Security Research: Rayner forms study*, Social and Community Planning Research for DHSS, London.

WEISBROD, B.A. (1970) *On the Stigma Affect and the Demand for Welfare Programmes – a Theoretical Note*, Institute for Research on Poverty, Discussion Paper 82-70, University of Wisconsin-Madison.

WHYLEY, C. and HUBY, M. (1993) *Take-up and the Social Fund: Applying the concept of take-up to a discretionary benefit*, JRF 1160, Social Policy Research Unit Working Paper, University of York.

WILLIAMS, T., ASTIN, M. and DITCH, J. (1995) *First Time Customers*, Department of Social Security Research Report Series No. 36, London: HMSO.

Index

Printed in the United Kingdom for HMSO
Dd.300913, 5/95, C12, 3396/4, 5673, 319847